T0157352

Out of the Ashes Came Hope

Lord, make me an instrument of Your peace.
Where there is hatred, let me sow love;
Where there is doubt, faith;
Where there is despair, hope;
Where there is darkness, light;
Where there is sadness, joy.

O, Divine Master,
Grant that I may not so much seek to be consoled as to console;
To be understood as to understand;
To be loved as to love;
For it is in giving that we receive;
It is in pardoning that we are pardoned;
It is in dying that we are born again to eternal life.

Out of the Ashes Came Hope

MONSIGNOR WILLIAM J. LINDER

WITH GILDA ROGERS

ARCHWAY
PUBLISHING

Copyright © 2016 William J. Linder.

All rights reserved. No part of this book may be used or reproduced by any means, graphic, electronic, or mechanical, including photocopying, recording, taping or by any information storage retrieval system without the written permission of the author except in the case of brief quotations embodied in critical articles and reviews.

This book is a work of non-fiction. Unless otherwise noted, the author and the publisher make no explicit guarantees as to the accuracy of the information contained in this book and in some cases, names of people and places have been altered to protect their privacy.

Archway Publishing books may be ordered through booksellers or by contacting:

Archway Publishing
1663 Liberty Drive
Bloomington, IN 47403
www.archwaypublishing.com
1 (888) 242-5904

Because of the dynamic nature of the Internet, any web addresses or links contained in this book may have changed since publication and may no longer be valid. The views expressed in this work are solely those of the author and do not necessarily reflect the views of the publisher, and the publisher hereby disclaims any responsibility for them.

Any people depicted in stock imagery provided by Thinkstock are models, and such images are being used for illustrative purposes only. Certain stock imagery © Thinkstock.

ISBN: 978-1-4808-3684-6 (sc)
ISBN: 978-1-4808-3683-9 (hc)
ISBN: 978-1-4808-3685-3 (e)

Library of Congress Control Number: 2016916424

Print information available on the last page.

Archway Publishing rev. date: 12/19/2016

Contents

Part I

Part II

Part III

FORWARD

By Craig Drinkard

I was a spry young teenager when my family moved into New Community Gardens Family Townhomes in October 1980. All the kids called where my family lived the "orange doors," because the various doors of the townhomes were painted in bright primary colors. That's where I first met Monsignor William Linder. He and other members of the New Community Corporation (NCC) team would often tour the grounds where we lived talking with the adults and kids about what the future of NCC looked like moving forward - more housing, a community recreation center and businesses. The housing complex where my family resided was the polar opposite of the low-income, subsidized housing that many of the original NCC founding members had lived in during the 1960's. Where we lived offered more than shelter. It actually provided a new paradigm for how low-income families were treated. NCC offered almost everything a family could ask for – access to social services, summer jobs for teens, along with recreational programs for the younger kids and an opportunity for families to nurture and care for their children in a decent and safe environment.

In my professional career today with the Victoria Foundation, one of NCC's longest private financial supporters providing over $8 million in grant funding, I began to spend time with a more reflective Monsignor Linder. Over time, we shared stories of our childhoods, empowering people often marginalized by the effects of racism, bad public policies, inadequate public education, and inept and corrupt elected officials. From these conversation spawned my insatiable desire to know the depth of Monsignor's journey, what he stood for, the history of the others who joined forces with him their accomplishments and why this work was so important.

This amazing journey of a freshly minted, baby-faced priest looking to intertwine his religious beliefs, while serving and empowering people is a triumphant showcase of honorable charity. The fate and faith of a young man from a working class family from Hudson County to becoming one of the "Faces of Hope" for the nation, was a remarkable feat. Monsignor's love for others transformed the lives of those routinely underserved in disinvested communities from Newark to Brooklyn, Chicago, and numerous cities around this country and across the globe.

Known as Father Linder back-in-the-day, he served God beyond his priestly title, collar, and pulpit. He learned that loving and serving God was best expressed by how one treated the most vulnerable people in society. And by doing so, he was relentless in his battle to elevate the dignity of those he was fighting for. Monsignor's story is an introspective winding path of self-reflection about how to best serve humanity. We see in his story how God makes paths for His work to be done through Monsignor's collaboration with loveable personalities from all walks of life.

Indeed, it was a strange mix of native *Newarkers*, who founded New Community Corporation, many living in public housing (some of the worst in the nation at the time), along with well-intentioned suburbanites, faith leaders, businessmen, and hard-working "everyday" types. They took on the audacious idea that New Jersey's largest city, Newark, could be transformed after the '67 Newark riots. Through their tireless efforts opportunities prevailed, from the first housing complex - New Community Homes Court - to nurturing childcare and educational facilities that empowered people to cultivate successful lives for themselves. For close to 50 years, New Community Corporation has put the needs of the people first. Under the umbrella of NCC, Babyland set the standard guidelines for infant daycare in the state, when it was established in 1969. Babyland also hired and first introduced me to the non-profit sector, by which I make a living today.

Often times we see successful individuals and marvel at their accomplishments – be it in business, politics, entertainment, sports, and even social change agents. Unfortunately, we fail to learn or inquire about their experiences, trials, setbacks, losses, small victories, people, and other transcending moments that ultimately shape their destiny. We get that opportunity in this memoir. Monsignor shares his life story against the back drop of his upbringing and how it all shaped his journey.

Introduction

The mobile police station was parked right outside the doors of the New Community Neighborhood Center on Hayes Street in Newark, New Jersey. A police officer greeted me as I exited the center, where the annual spring festival was going on, and walked me to my car.

"Monsignor it was a light night in the city. Only one homicide," he said, before I opened my car door.

"That's all?" I responded, surprised. It was not unusual to have four, five or even six homicides on a given night in Newark. "I pray they'll be no more," I said, as I got into my car and drove off. On the ride home, my mind wandered over the ebb and flow of life's terrain, where the human spirit eventually collides with revelation, redemption and salvation - that one defining moment - when all hope is restored.

Eventually, there comes a time when a person must wonder: *What am I here for? What lessons have I learned along the way that my life might best reflect humanity for humanity's sake?* There is no denying that living in Newark for 50 years has given my life real purpose and meaning. However, my love of service to others is what gives me strength.

I returned to my car to head home. The stoplight turned green and I slowly accelerated past a pristine neighborhood block, now a diminutive replica of what it used to be. There wasn't any sign of the bars, pimps, prostitutes, or hustlers that once christened the street their Broadway. A world that Nathan C. Heard wrote about in his gritty novel, *Howard Street*. The author's own redemption tells us about life's ebb and flow. While serving a prison sentence during the '60, Nathan Heard wrote a book that clearly exposed the underbelly of the black human condition. Later, he wound up teaching creative writing at Rutgers University.

Since those days, Newark's Central Ward has come to be known for its institutions of higher learning – Rutgers University, Essex County College and The New Jersey Institute of Technology, along with the Rutgers Biomedical Health Sciences School (formerly the University of Medicine and Dentistry of New Jersey) and Seton Hall Law School. And smack dab in the middle of this is New Community Corporation (NCC), comprised of 12 housing developments spread throughout Newark's Central and West Wards, as well as in the cities of Orange and Jersey City. Also under the umbrella of NCC is a healthcare facility, shopping center, the Workforce Development Center, along with corporate facilities, a recreation community center, credit union, early childhood learning centers, adult education and community resource centers, and more.

People now come from around the world to tour New Community developments. Among them have been heads of state, like Archbishop Desmond Tutu from South Africa and Princess Beatrix of the Netherlands. Both of whom marveled at what they saw. New Community's accomplishments have garnered both national and international acclaim. It is recognized as one of the largest community development corporation in the United States, as well as, New Jersey's largest non-profit housing corporation with net assets worth $300 million.

I lived through Newark's turmoil, witnessing both the revolution and the evolution of ideas that changed the city from a racist political power structure to a place where hope could thrive. Amid very chaotic experiences, the young people have made all the difference in Newark. I, too, was young then, and the adrenaline that fueled my actions to reject the abject racist and corrupt construct of the city was placed upon my heart by God. As a result, I made my share of enemies. People whose contempt for me has sometimes worked against New Community Corporation. But that's the reality that comes with change. Like Chicago Mayor Richard Daly, who had a way of getting things done for the good of the city, but wasn't always deemed a fair person by all people. I, too, have received my share of harsh criticism from people.

However, my biggest concern these days isn't with someone who disagrees with me, but rather the fact that we're losing our young people at record rates. There's more black-on-black crime than ever before. In the black community, the violence has become normalized and, over time, accepted. And in the larger white community, as long as it's black-on-black it's okay.

Back in 1962, before I came to Newark, when I was still studying at the seminary, I wrote a research paper for my Sociology class about Newark and its issues. What really got my attention was the number of deaths of people in their 20's. As a seminarian, I had access to information found in the coroner's report listing them as having died from a heart attack, which technically was true. But what had caused these heart attacks? I discovered that it was drugs. Drugs rule today as the culprit that has led to the proliferation of the violence we see happening here in Newark. The lack of decent paying jobs, if you ask me, is what leads to an underground economy fueled by drugs. The schools are in shambles and these are problems that need to be confronted and dealt with honestly and efficiently.

The blatant racism and corruption that has too often defined Newark still manages to outshine the potential of the city's people. The most ludicrous thing I've heard in a long time occurred in Camden, New Jersey, where a decision was made to privatize the police force to shave millions of dollars off the budget. How could a city riddled with crime abolish their own police department and bring in an outside enforcement agency to save money? What does that say about our society? That human life is really not that important. The potential of the people is again being ignored.

Who would think that we'd still be grappling with poverty in the 21st Century? Although I realize that's the cyclical nature of life itself - that doesn't change – people do – as was the case with Nathan C. Heard. It is up to the people to change the poverty situation. Through good deeds and honest dialogue and conversation we can shape the best of humanity in trying times. I worry about the time it will take before a rising tide of hope comes ashore to awaken our senses again to the fact that we're all in this boat together. It's up to all of us to change what ails society today.

That was the beauty of the Civil Rights Movement. The restorative nature of the time made it significant. The seeds of hope and resilience spread across this nation and brought us all together in a culminating moment of greatness that began to change humanity and heal our nation. I am hopeful that poverty will be eradicated. Maybe not in my lifetime. But I will remain hopeful. That's just how I see the world. Hope is the most spontaneous prayer that exists.

PART I

CHAPTER ONE

A City in Crisis: The '67 Summer Disorders

Yes, I know how many are your crimes, how grievous your sins: Oppressing the just, accepting bribes, turning away the needy at the gate - Amos 5:12

All that had been was now gone in the Central Ward. The exception to the destruction was the all-black parish, Queen of Angels Church, located on Belmont Avenue that stood on the backside of the newly constructed West Kinney Junior High School. Every window in the school got smashed. But not a single window at Queen of Angels, or any other part of the building, had been touched.

It was apparent that there was selectivity in the actions of those wreaking havoc. No other street illustrated this more clearly than Springfield Avenue, where a number of furniture stores were located. The stores were all burned to the ground with the exception, once again, of just one. The store left standing had a good reputation and sold expensive, excellent quality furniture. Unlike the other furniture establishments, this store did not operate on high-interest credit plans and focused instead on lay-away plans. The owners catered to the people in the community, thus the store had been spared. The tension in the city had boiled over. When things finally simmered down on July 18, 1967, over 1,000 people were injured and 26 people were dead. There was also untold property loss and damage escalating into the millions of dollars.

The 1967 Summer Disorders, as it was labeled by the Lilley Commission, instead of "riots," struck the city of Newark like a rip-roaring hurricane destroying everything in its path. Formally known as "The Governor's Select Commission on Civil Disorders," this body became more widely known as the Lilley Commission, named after Robert Lilley, CEO of New Jersey Bell Telephone Company, who was appointed chairman by Governor Richard Hughes.

Six months after the unrest, in February of 1968, the commission delivered a thorough report to the governor that pointed to a wide-range of factors that precipitated the six-day war between the powerless black residents of Newark and the city's powerful white political structure. One of the more potent findings revealed an insidious culture of corruption that loomed large over New Jersey's largest city.

Three witnesses who testified before the commission shared a similar message that had come to define Newark: There is a price for everything at city hall. The Summer Disorders exposed the corrupt nature of the political power that ruled the city. The white men who were entrusted to lead and protect Newark were addicted to power. They were no different than any hoodlums, thugs and gangsters roaming the streets looking to get their next high. The only difference was that they wore suits, ties and police uniforms.

In 1962, Hugh J. Addonizio was elected as Newark's 33rd mayor. Addonizio's approach to the "Negro," the identifying term used at the time for black people, was as paternal as it was progressive. During his seven terms in the United States House of Representatives, he consistently voted for progressive civil rights legislation. To some of his critics, Addonizio's gambling problem superseded his mayoral capabilities.

Drunk with power, Addonizio and his gang of henchmen in the police department seemingly failed to see the knock-out punch coming – the '67 Summer Disorders. It was evident in his statement made before the Lilley Commission. "I don't care if a Negro sat here as mayor," he said smugly. "He couldn't do anything more for the Negro than I've done."

During his campaign for a second mayoral term in 1966, Addonizio's campaign dubbed as "Program for a Better Newark" made the headlines in the *New Jersey Afro American* newspaper. He called for school reform, ending segregation and discrimination, and appointing a commission to strengthen race relations in the city. Addonizio's campaign took out full-page ads in black-owned newspapers where he boasted that unemployment had been "cut in half" under his administration. These tactics garnered a deeper loyalty among black residents and secured Addonizio a second term as mayor of Newark. Even after he was convicted of corruption on September 22, 1970, for allegedly taking $1.4 million in kick-backs from land development deals, prominent black religious leaders still supported him. Meanwhile, the quality of life for blacks in Newark had worsened in critical areas such as housing and employment opportunities.

Newark had once been an industrial powerhouse and was home to the Westinghouse plant, leading the way in the field of electronics, to breweries, dairies and Tiffany & Co. in North Newark. As the demand for jobs grew among the black population, the number of manufacturing jobs declined – from 96,000 jobs in 1952 down to 54,000 in 1972. Private businesses still resisted hiring black workers. The overwhelming perception that blacks were unreliable employees or, worse, lazy, led to a lack of jobs for low-skilled black workers. Blacks and Puerto Ricans were shut out of construction jobs, while low-skilled white workers went home with a paycheck at week's end.

Meanwhile, the Newark Police Department's outright prejudice toward the black community effectively promoted Jim Crow, north of the Mason Dixon line. In a city where the black population was more than 50 percent by 1966, the same diversity was not reflected in the mere number of 145 black police officers on the roster compared to 1,322 white officers. Power remained in the hands of a corrupt white police brass. Even the police director had allegations linking him to the "numbers" and drug rackets. There was no balance of power for the growing black population. The principle of democratic participation in Newark's local government was relatively non-existent for blacks.

By this time, Newark had become the nation's poster child for the highest rate of substandard housing. From a list of 1,409 tenement apartment buildings and rooming houses, 1,300 units were deemed substandard. Many units had no running water, working toilets or central heat. Newark was comprised of five distinct wards and the highest concentration of blacks – some 53,000 residents – were corralled in the

Central Ward. Many of them were subjected to substandard housing or were stacked atop one another in high-rise public housing buildings. Most of the poorly constructed wood-framed houses available had been built around 1910, without plumbing. Later on, plumbing got added with the addition of bathrooms in enclosed back porches. Black tenants paid extraordinarily high rents to slumlords, whose consciences registered as being out-of-order, just like the plumbing in most of their dilapidated houses.

The black community lived within a culture of corruption and was subjected to police brutality at whim. As a result, tensions began to rise. Frustration sprung from many sources but foremost from a lack of control in local affairs. For example, the "numbers" was a combination of digits derived from legalized horse racing – win, place and show – that one could bet on daily, similar to the lottery. To "hit" the number provided an economic boost to the black community's pocketbook. Blacks supplied the runners and had some numbers banks, but the heartbeat of the operation pulsed elsewhere, under white control, and ultimately lined those pockets.

A parishioner from Queen of Angels Church, where I was assigned as a priest, actually went to jail for a couple of years after authorities accused her of operating a numbers bank. Only white people were privy to an "escape clause" and avoided being penalized for unlawful crimes. That clause obviously didn't apply to the black woman who went to jail.

During the mid to late '60s, Newark ranked second in the nation when it came to crime and infant mortality. Black women who were unwed mothers or foster mothers faced exclusion from public housing, according to the report by the Lilley Commission. And if a child was born out of wedlock to a black woman while she lived in public housing, she risked eviction. A number of these women worked as domestics in the surrounding suburbs such as Montclair, Millburn and West Orange. Many of these women were subjected to unstable situations regarding the care of their children while at work, which contributed, at times, to poor work attendance. The lack of affordable infant daycare centers posed a significant hardship for low-income mothers and families.

When it came to public schools, by 1966 a number of the elementary schools in Newark were all black, with as many as 40 students per classroom. Once an academic bastion of preparing white students for college, Weequahic High School had shifted to 70 percent black. Newark resident Regina Marshall was among those students. A member of the Catholic Youth Organization at Queen of Angels, Regina had applied to Weequahic High as an out-of-district student. Her sights were set on attending college and she wanted to study Hebrew. Her district school, South Side High School (now called Malcolm X Shabazz), did not offer that course, which made her eligible to attend Weequahic High. Regina excelled in Hebrew, speaking, writing and reading the language fluently. She was the first black student to receive an award for excellence in Hebrew upon graduation in 1967. Before then, the award had not been bestowed upon anyone since 1942. In 2006 Dr. Regina Marshall Adesanya became the chairperson of the Early Childhood Education Department at New Jersey City University.

When given an opportunity, most children will succeed in life. However, the decrepit school facilities in Newark dating back more than a hundred years, with windows replaced by wooden two-by-fours, didn't give a child much semblance of hope. Using such a crude looking board to replace a broken window in an elementary school in upscale Montclair would have been unacceptable, I am certain.

As far as the school's demographics, black teachers were greatly outnumbered by their white peers, despite the makeup of the majority black student body. There were a total of 3,500 white teachers and a little more than 800 black teachers. Several black teachers received a temporary teacher certification, while others only held a substitute teacher certification. From the outset, their path to achieving a permanent tenured teaching position was filled with obstacles. Not one black school principal oversaw a school in the entire district.

The politics of Addonizio's administration also loomed large over education in the city. The mayor exercised influence through his allies, who ran the labor unions. The unions, a powerfully persuasive brotherhood in rank and file, effectively controlled the Newark Board of Education. But things were about to change.

The years 1966 and 1967 were pivotal turning points in Black

America. The rising tide of Black Nationalism erupted with the Black Panthers and their strong political stance against the status quo. Though I am not an advocate of violence, I believe their defiance was necessary at the time. They were devoted to saving their people. Not everyone was receptive to Dr. King's message of nonviolence. I found myself drawn to the Panthers' rhetoric of self-determination, and how they were trained and policed their community. The Black Panthers played a crucial role in this country's social development.

I believe these social advances prepared America for Diahann Carroll, who starred on primetime television in "Julia," in a non-stereotypical role for a black actress, as a nurse, and Greg Morris, as the technical-scientific wizard of the crew in "Mission Impossible." In 1967, Sidney Poitier graced the silver screen in "Guess Who's Coming to Dinner" and "To Sir with Love." Both films served as a social commentary and chronicled the country's tumultuous transformation through humor and drama. Musically, there was the Queen of Soul, Aretha Franklin, who summed it up best with R-E-S-P-E-C-T. And Motown was "The sound of young America." Finally, the black race took its long overdue, but rightful, place at the forefront of mainstream American culture. These powerful black images and voices, like Harry Belafonte who spoke out against social injustice, were significant outcries against the status quo.

The same collective energy that was infiltrating all sectors of society was pulsating in Newark. By 1967, the black community had found its voice. In a highly controversial issue that involved a vacant seat for the official position of secretary on the Board of Education, the black community held the mayor's feet to the fire. In 1967, black residents and organizations, both militant and otherwise, made 92 appearances at the school board meetings. The presence of the black community at school board meetings had more than quadrupled from a dismal 22 appearances the year before. Key organizations like the Congress of Racial Equality, also called CORE, and ONE (Organization for Negro Educators) were in support of Wilbur Parker, the first black certified public accountant in Newark and the city's budget director – for the school board Secretary position.

However, Addonizio played his usual power politics and appointed his friend, Councilman James Callaghan, to fill the vacant secretary seat, although Callaghan didn't possess a high school diploma. Clearly, Parker was the more qualified candidate for the position. But this time, Addonizio's power politics went nowhere, because the black community had had enough.

The mayor's actions set in motion a runaway train that was fueled by an extremely agitated community. There were meetings I attended, where the seething anger that emanated from the crowd would have left the average person deathly afraid. Usually, I was the only white person in the room. Those who were running the meeting, after ranting about what they would do to this white person or that white person, would then respectfully turn to me and ask, "Would you like to come up and say a few words?"

But even wilder was the day of reckoning, when the runaway train derailed and crashed. On July 12, 1967, at Newark's Fourth Police Precinct located in the Central Ward, a taxicab driver named John Smith was booked and charged with resisting arrest, assault and battery. It was here that he was severely beaten and sustained injuries that warranted medical attention. It was here that the residents peering out from the windows of the nearby 12-story Hayes Homes projects witnessed the scuffle. It was here that all the disrespect, disillusionment and disregard endured by the black community met in a head-on collision with Newark's white political power structure. It was here at the Fourth Police Precinct that the black community rose up because they had nothing to lose. And that's when all hell broke loose.

The predominately all white police force took the opportunity to retaliate against the black community. That's when the situation turned into an all-out war. Peering out of the windows from Queen of Angels Church, Monsignor Thomas Carey and I spotted a black man with an arm full of groceries. After the patrol car pulled up beside him, the white officers got out and seized the man's bags and threw them down, causing all his food to spill onto the ground. Monsignor Carey rushed out with bags to help the man so that he could be on his way before something tragic happened.

The Newark police failed to control the marauding crowds. Despite being sworn to "protect and serve," Newark police ran as wild in the streets as the other looters dashing in and out of stores. Their actions served as unspoken permission for the young people to follow suit.

Bullets whizzing through the air stopped looters dead in their tracks, along with innocent bystanders who were also laid to rest. Gangs of young black males walked down the streets in defiance, chanting, "These are our streets now." It was an assertion of power that they had never before wielded. Years of pent up anger and frustration now was recklessly on full display.

In the midst of the chaos, I transported people to and from the hospital in my Volkswagen Beetle. City Hospital was used for the community and St. Michael's Hospital was where firemen and policemen were taken. At some point it dawned on me that no one was controlling the outcome of what was happening. This was not an organized rebellion. It was raging like the wildfires of California, with no end in sight. Caught in the fray of it, I hadn't given much thought to being afraid.

The African-American leadership at the time proved to be utterly ineffective. No one listened to them. Many of them didn't even live in the area. Their leadership was bankrupt, along with folks like Irvine Turner, who was tied to the whole political scene downtown, which severely compromised him. As the first black Newark councilman, Turner moved in lockstep with Addonizio's political machine, so much so that Turner, along with others, was indicted in the corruption scandal that sent Addonizio to federal prison in 1970.

It was evident after 24 hours of total insurrection that the Newark Police Department could not control the madness. They were replaced by state troopers, who swooped in ready to save the day but instead got their butts beat pretty badly. They were quickly overwhelmed by the level of disorder. I could see they had never seen anything like this before and, quite frankly, neither had I. The police cars ripping and roaring down the streets, with their sirens blaring, only fueled the pandemonium.

Soon thereafter, the National Guard rolled into the city and occupied it in armored trucks and Army tanks, seemingly more suited for

Vietnam. I remember looking at the faces of two of the guards, as they rolled down the streets in their armored trucks and thinking, *these are kids.* In fact, in the aftermath, a number of innocent deaths would be attributed to them. They weren't trained and you could see it; they were frightened to death. In one such case, a woman was simply trying to close the window at the housing project where she lived and was met with a spray of bullets that took her life.

It was the Newark Fire Department whose valor during the six-day melee that I most admired. People were engulfed in fear as plumes of smoke filled the heavens. In an act of tremendous bravery with bullets still whizzing by, Newark Fire Chief John Caufield stood on the top rung of his ladder, visible to his men, risking his life so that his subordinates would not flee the scene. That kind of leadership kept the unit together. While under sniper fire, Caufield got in there with his men to extinguish fires. Given the situation, I don't think that too many people would have shown that kind of bravery.

The fires eventually burned out and the deadly storm of bullets ended. The streets were quiet. The people had exerted their power. It was as if they said, "Hey, now we need to begin again, start over."

The Fourth Police Precinct, near what is now Irvine Turner Boulevard, was the center of the summer disturbances in July 1967.

CHAPTER 2

Queen of Angels: My *Lilies of the Field*

*Ask and it will be given to you; seek and you will find; knock
and the door will be opened* – Matthew 7:7

I had been assigned to serve at Queen of Angels Church in 1963. I called ahead to announce my arrival only to discover the telephone had been disconnected. Dressed in a suit, I showed up on a Saturday in early June ready to report for duty. Monsignor Thomas Carey, the administrative pastor at the church, took me around and introduced me to everybody. We went out back where the men of the church were digging a ditch. Queen of Angels was an old German parish that dated back to the 1850s and its infrastructure was terribly outdated. The church did not have a storm sewer system and the men were working to install one in the back of the church, where the children from the Queen of Angels parochial school played. The area was filled with gravel, which helped to absorb the rainwater but caused the children to skin their knees often during recess. There was no heavy duty equipment on site to make the job easier. To my surprise, these men were manually digging the ground with shovels and pickaxes, breaking through years and years of rock formation to install a sewer system. It was on the site of this massive project where I met Joe Chaneyfield.

"We work around this place. You ain't doing us no good standing there with your little suit on. Everybody works, priests and all," he said. Broad and truncated, Joe cut an imposing figure. I took his cue and went to change my clothes. After I did, he welcomed my return.

"Oh you're back and gotcha work clothes on," he said, chuckling. "What's your name again?"

"Father Linder."

"Okay, Father Linder. Grab a shovel and let me see what you can do," he said.

I have come to trust and believe that life experiences have a way of preparing you for what's up ahead. I was in relatively good physical shape and was able to work as hard as Joe and the other workers. I was grateful for all the summers that I had worked in construction with my uncles and lifting weights while at the seminary, because Joe wasn't joking around when it came to doing physical labor. In those grueling four hours, he and I formed the beginning of a friendship and a brotherhood that would withstand the test of time.

Digging alongside these men from the church felt like an initiation of sorts. I couldn't have asked for a better introduction, because I got to know them on an informal basis, which made me more of an equal to them, rather than someone of superiority as their new priest. In all the muck and mire that we tossed above our heads, we hallowed a place for trust and understanding to flourish.

The new black tenants at Queen of Angels were refurbishing the church and calling it their own. There had been a small group of black Catholics in Newark dating back to the 1920s. As a matter of fact, poet and activist Amiri Baraka's mother, Anna Jones, belonged to Queen of Angels in the early years. The majority of parishioners at the church came from the Central Ward housing projects—either the Stella Wright and Hayes Homes, or the Scudder Homes in Newark. Queen of Angels was within walking distance to all three. Ninety percent of the parishioners were new to the Catholic religion, which, for me, made the atmosphere truly thrilling because there was a cross-section of ideas emerging.

The year 1963 was a dynamic time at the church. A few months after my arrival, *Lilies of the Field,* starring Sidney Poitier, debuted in movie theaters. Poitier won an Oscar for his role as Homer Smith, a character who stumbled upon a group of East German nuns who want to build a chapel for the community. When I saw the movie, Poitier's portrayal of Smith reminded me of what I was experiencing at Queen of Angels.

Not only had the men installed a massive sewer system, they had also rebuilt the parochial school. I worked alongside them painting the rectory. It was a work in progress that we worked on a little at a time. Much like Poitier and the nuns who worked together to build their chapel, everyone helped out in the effort to aesthetically resurrect the church. The difference at Queen of Angels were the four white priests – Thomas Carey, Joe Staub, Willie Yeo and myself – among all black parishioners. We fully adopted the church and transformed it from the parish it once was to a new church with a fresh outlook for the community.

We were in this together. A swirling spirit of camaraderie, love and respect for one another graced our parish and sealed our commitment to it. This was our "amen" moment and our up-tempo beat was just as lively as the song that Poitier and the nuns sang together in the movie. All of our hard work paid off and the beauty was we'd done it without a power hierarchy. I typically dressed in work clothes and as a result, one of the nuns at the church didn't even know I was a priest there until two months later. We were working together in harmony. Amen!

Each priest had varying roles at the church. Under Monsignor Carey's leadership as the presiding pastor, Queen of Angels earned national prominence. Carey didn't place many restrictions on us regarding what we were allowed to do. He understood the needs of the community. Queen of Angels garnered national coverage for its involvement in civil rights and had the reputation of being a progressive church. Joe Staub was mostly involved in education with the parochial school and worked with the younger children. Willie Yeo lent him a hand and also worked with the men of the church. I gravitated towards the "social action" side of what was happening in the community. My interest in sociology led me in that direction. I worked closely with the teenagers of the parish. Early on, my mission was to get the young people involved in pressing matters that involved the deplorable housing conditions in the city's Central Ward. I also trained them in community organizing. It was important that their voices be heard. Many of them were high school and college students eager to embrace new ideas.

Creativity and new ideas flowed at Queen of Angels. Even as Newark struggled with turmoil, it was an exciting time to be coming up. We knew that change was on the way. The church formed a coalition to fight the corruption and politics that was designed to keep black people locked out of the power structure and locked, historically, in "their place." The verve from this collective consciousness was the most intriguing and puzzling paradox I could have ever imagined - the joy of the community was as visceral as its pain, with a ray of hope wedged somewhere in between.

The continuing agony of the Black community hit the church hard, when about two weeks after my arrival on June 12, 1963, civil rights leader Medgar Evers was gunned down and killed in his driveway by white assailants. I felt the pain and this drew me to the movement.

One of my first assignments when I got to Queen of Angels was to organize the church's participation in the 1963 March on Washington. I was happy to take on the leadership role. I wanted to get involved in something big as I sought to be an obedient servant of the Lord. I'll never forget the joyful celebration as 150 people boarded three DeCamp buses at 5 a.m. in front of the church, headed to Washington, D.C. Together we were embarking on a journey. The aroma that emanated from the fried chicken sandwiches, pound cake, and sweet potato pie stuffed in aluminum foil-lined shoe boxes was enough to wake up the taste buds early that morning.

As we made our way onto the New Jersey Turnpike, the interstate was packed with caravans of buses. By the time we reached Philadelphia, our Newark delegation was in fine form. They were singing gospel hymns as we waved vigorously at others on their way down to the historic event.

Once we arrived in Washington, D.C. and disembarked, we merged with the enormous crowd swell and were swept away by excitement and anticipation. Seeing all the interracial activity was a glorious sight, especially for those people coming from the South. Black and white, young and old, Baptists, Catholics, Jews, Methodists and Protestants and others of various religious and ethnic persuasions all made their way onto the mall, where the Rev. Dr. Martin Luther King Jr. was to appear.

Then came the moment when King stood before us. The tenor of his Baptist preaching roots reverberated through the mall as he eloquently delivered a message that forever changed our lives. He wasn't big in stature but he represented a towering symbol of hope. He effectively tied the religious and social arenas together in an altruistic manner that all of us were able to walk away feeling as if we had been in the presence of greatness.

Even now, I must admit that no one could have told me on that hot August day that an African-American man named Barack Obama would be elected president of the United States in 2008. No way, that was just too far out. But King's words of hope magnified even more what is possible. And the fact that Obama was re-elected in 2012 *is* what change looks like.

The March on Washington personally moved me and fueled even greater expectations for change in Newark. It was all about creating relationships and getting to know the people in the community and showing them that I was someone who meant well.

Joe Chaneyfield, who by now had become like a brother to me, was the founder and president of the first independent union of Maintenance Workers Local 305 AFL-CIO. The laborers, who were a part of the union, would pick up their paychecks, at what I called the "maintenance cribs" in the basement at Scudder Homes. When they came I was there to extend them a handshake and brief conversation. That's how I got to know these men really well.

"Hey Tank how's it going?"

"Big Eddie who you going with in the big fight, Liston or Clay?"

"Oh I'm bettin' on Clay," said Big Eddie enthusiastically. "How 'bout you?"

"Well if I were a betting ... "

"Oh Father Linder, please forgive me," said Eddie, who was naturally embarrassed, forgetting I was a priest. Waging a bet of this kind wasn't part of my repertoire.

"Forget about it," I replied with a wave of my hand. "I'm banking my prayer on Clay. Don't worry. I got you covered." We couldn't help but laugh.

Then there were somber times when my priest's collar offered solace to a family during the Vietnam War. It wasn't unusual for me to receive a telephone call from a representative of the United States Marine Corps requesting that I accompany the Marines to one of the housing projects to deliver the news that a loved one was a "casualty of war." This scene always made me reflect on the anxiety that I had felt when my uncles were fighting in WWII. When someone opens the door and sees that full formal dress Marine uniform, you don't have to say anything. My uncles returned home safe from the war. Yet, it was something about that experience that crystallized for me the paradox of love and war. Like Mother Teresa said, "If you love until it hurts, there can be no more hurt, only more love." I hoped that my presence was a sign of God's love for them as they heard the grim news.

I also made my rounds to Black owned businesses, including bars and taverns. Located near the Stella Wright Homes, the Alcazar Bar located at 72 Waverly Ave. (later renamed Muhammad Ali Ave.), was run by Pop Durham and was a hotbed of activity. It was the "happening" neighborhood watering hole. To compensate for its lackluster interior, the Alcazar Bar drew a gathering of free thinkers, such as musicians and those who engaged in nonviolent, progressive dialogue. If you wanted to find out what was going on you went down to the Alcazar Bar. But the bar was also a place where I could get support for the movement. On many of my visits, I'd be there collecting money for the Freedom Riders, who were traveling on buses going down South to participate in voter registration drives.

Honestly, for me to witness the unraveling of the 1965 Voting Rights Act by the Supreme Court in 2013, not only confirms the cyclical nature of history, but ought to serve as a "call to action." Every generation is called into existence to advance humanity. This one is no different. The Court has invited people to raise up against the voter suppression laws that are sweeping across the nation, since rendering its decision. To see the most historically marginalized populations being denied full access to the right to vote in the 21st Century is pretty unbelievable. These voter suppression laws run counter to our democracy and despite what the Court has said, the people will eventually enact change just as we did. That's what we're seeing now in the "Black Lives Matter" Movement, with the opposition labeling them as trouble makers. They're no more trouble makers than we were. These young people are fed up with the status quo of unarmed black men and boys being shot and killed. And in most cases no one is held accountable for their deaths.

The way things changed in Newark had a lot to do with organizations like the Urban League. It had a large and active office right in the Central Ward. CORE (Congress of Racial Equality), although a smaller outfit than the Urban League, run by Bob Curvin, was more aggressive and action-oriented. Members of CORE would unexpectedly show up and demonstrate at construction sites, in protest over the lack of black workers. They seemed to be doing more in respect to improving opportunities for black workers than Addonizio's quasi "Equal Employment Opportunity Committee."

This surge of activism and the non-violent tenor of the Civil Rights Movement were a natural fit. To be a part of this youthful grassroots uprising was one of the greatest times in my life. To be involved in this monumental humanitarian adventure, while dubious about the outcome, made it even more exciting. The power to change this nation for the better was in the hands of the people. The lawmakers had no choice but to follow suit. The Civil Rights Movement in all its glory was democracy operating at its best in the worst of times. I look back now and feel very privileged and lucky to have wound up in Newark at that particular time.

Naturally, when the opportunity presented itself for me to travel down South to participate in the march from Selma to Montgomery, I jumped right on it. I informed Monsignor Carey that I was going to Alabama and no sooner than I did, he immediately notified Archbishop Thomas Boland of the Diocese of Newark. The archbishop relayed the message that it was my right of conscience to do that, although he wasn't enthusiastic about my trip. In truth, I was not actually asking for permission to go. I was going regardless of what either one of them said.

Once in Selma, my colleagues and I were expecting to pay a visit to the archbishop of the Diocese in Alabama. But we were curtly informed that the archbishop didn't want anything to do with us "meddling" white northern priests. He never did receive us. I was a part of the third attempt to march from Selma to Montgomery on March 21, 1965. The first march, more infamously known as "Bloody Sunday," was led by United States Congressman John Lewis, who, along with 500 marchers, was viciously attacked by a band of Alabama state troopers, on the Edmund Pettus Bridge. The second attempt was thwarted and the marchers were turned around at the bottom of the bridge.

This time around, the march was successful and we arrived in Montgomery on March 25, 1965. There were thousands of people along the 50-mile stretch to Montgomery, and I could see tears streaming down many of their faces, especially the elderly in the crowd. You have to remember in Lowndes County, where we passed through, the black population was over 80 percent and there was not one black person registered to vote. The only people in that county who voted were white. For those elders in that county to witness so many young Black Americans, alongside those of us who were white, marching together for voting rights and equality for black people was like seeing one of God's miracles unfold right before their eyes. The absurdity that people could not exercise their right to vote because of race was unconscionable, to me.

Over 100 years after the Civil War and despite President Abraham Lincoln having signed the Emancipation Proclamation in 1863, we continued to experience a form of "slavery." The fortitude it took to turn an amoral white social construct right-side up was explosive. Scores of lives lost just so people could be treated with dignity. People were still fighting to death. Frederick Douglass, the great abolitionist and advisor to President Lincoln, knew it would be a long hard fought battle but was optimistic in his resolve. His words became my mantra: *Without struggle there is no progress.*

When we crossed the Edmund Pettus Bridge on our trek to Montgomery, I was inspired by the endless possibilities of building bridges between the black and white races once I got back to Newark. But what I found so fascinating was the great number of young people, mere teenagers, who were trained as marshals and organizers of the march. They were the ones who instructed the white priests and nuns to flank the outside of the lines, which was really smart, because the opposition would not be so quick to react. The passing of the Civil Rights Act in 1964 and the Voting Rights Act in 1965 spelled progress, but there was still so much more work to be done.

CHAPTER 3

The Idea for a New Community

In every way I have shown you that by hard work of that sort we must help the weak, and keep in mind the words of the Lord Jesus who himself said, 'It is more blessed to give than to receive'" - Acts 20:35

Five ethnically diverse wards make up the city of Newark. Within each isolated enclave, each group can act as if no one exists other than themselves. Mayor Hugh Addonizio's aggressive urban renewal process started in 1964 and served to further perpetuate this isolation. The city ran what is now Interstate 280 as a wall to north Newark to keep that side of the city white, mostly Italian. The lower part of the South Ward, which was still Jewish, had the protective shield of Interstate 78 from outsiders. The East Ward, known as the Ironbound section, was comprised of Portuguese and Spanish speaking people and they were secluded on their side of the city. The West Ward was mostly black.

However, the largest concentration of Black residents lived in the Central Ward, where the city in the grand scheme of eminent domain had taken over 200 acres of land for the proposed University of Medicine and Dentistry of New Jersey. The amount of land was eventually reduced to about 155 acres, with Rutgers University and the New Jersey Institute of Technology each receiving an additional 25 acres. The city also allocated 25 acres to Seton Hall University, but Seton Hall chose to keep its location in South Orange and instead established its law school in Newark.

Urban renewal was just one part of Addonizio's plan for a new Newark. He also proposed establishing a two-year junior college.

However, that institution that is now Essex County College almost didn't happen. Most of the white county officials wanted the college to be located in West Essex, among the more affluent suburbs.

Harry Lerner, the chairman of the Democratic Party in Essex County at the time, was responsible for keeping the much needed institution of higher learning in the heart of Newark, in the Central Ward. In 1964, Harry made sure that I was appointed to the committee that was formed to discuss the planning of the proposed college. Harry had been a cab driver and was partial to Newark. He detested the idea that the Essex County College could possibly be hi-jacked to the suburbs. He wanted me in the mix, because he knew of my conviction for social justice and my involvement with the Black community. The proposed college was a great incentive for Black people living in the Central Ward to access higher education.

Around that same time, I met Zachary Yamba, a native of Ghana who was doing his undergraduate work at Seton Hall University. In 1968, when Essex County College opened, Zach joined the faculty there. He often stopped by Queen of Angels where we had engaging conversations and over time the church became his second home. He had a keen intellect and possessed a kind and gentlemanly demeanor. In the late '70s, Essex County College was on the brink of losing its academic accreditation and almost shutting its doors. Zach, who by then had become a dear friend, was named president of Essex County College in 1980. It was his vision and the guiding principles of integrity, independence and commitment that saved the school from its demise. We had fought hard to get the school in the Central Ward and I was grateful for Zack's leadership in resurrecting the school to the respectable institution that it is today and increasing student enrollment.

Meanwhile, Addonizio's urban renewal plan meant that people were forced out of their homes and offered few options for replacement housing. The city's housing authority did a poor job of communicating this to the thousands of displaced residents in the Central Ward. The city didn't seem to care about the welfare of its black residents when it came to providing an alternative plan for housing. The sheer expression of desperation that I saw on the faces of people at Sunday Mass or out on the streets infiltrated my very being.

I was growing as a priest. The gospel of love ran wild in me and I was possessed by an urgency to restore hope to what looked like a hopeless situation. Imagine being faced with nowhere to live. The uncertainty and anguish I was witnessing was heartbreaking. The people and I were joined by the Eucharist and Holy Communion, God the Father, the Son and the Holy Spirit. But I walked such a fine line between the secular and religious worlds. One could have defined my behavior back then as an overzealous messenger of God's love or as being radically insane. I chose not to fear the improbable.

The year was 1965 and the zeitgeist of the time led singer and songwriter, Curtis Mayfield to pen the song, "People Get Ready," that played like an anthem in my head. "People get ready, there's a train comin'/ You don't need no baggage, you just get on board/All you need is faith to hear the diesels hummin'/You don't need no ticket you just thank the Lord."

Though I had given up the idea of being an engineer when I decided to become a priest, I still remained intrigued by the operational science of civil engineering – how design and the environment could work in harmony. My strong aptitude in construction was the result of having worked during the summers while still in high school on construction sites with my uncles. Call it a brief moment of illumination, but the notion to build a city within a city was possible to me. The path I had chosen, as a priest, had everything to do with "social engineering."

"All Aboard."

My lofty vision – to build a city within a city – opened an exchange of ideas that eagerly flowed between Joe Chaneyfield, Willie Wright and me about what our new community could be. When the unthinkable happened – the '67 Summer Disorders – we had a chance to build in the Central Ward and put our money where our mouths were. The stench from buildings set on fire still lingered in the air for months. Brick and mortar reduced to debris and rubble were visible as far as the eye could see up Springfield Avenue. The Central Ward was barren and nearly decimated. The question of whether the Central Ward could be built back up never came up – it had to be. There was nothing left but darkness and despair.

The unraveling mystery of events that landed me in Newark now revealed the missionary work that I had longed to do when I entered the seminary. The Jesuits' allegiance to foreign missionary work held a certain attraction for me in the past. I was romanced by the idea of going to foreign lands to help dig wells, build houses and perhaps even teach. What I was looking for was not in some far away land, but rather right here. What was once a conundrum for me was now clear: To be a servant of God and to all His people was my destiny.

Some of the members of Queen of Angels, particularly Joe and Willie, we started conducting organizational meetings for what eventually became New Community Corporation. The meetings centered on defining the role the community would play in the rebuilding process. The men were particularly interested in building housing, while the women were concerned about daycare for children. Over the course of two years, these topics would arise at many meetings. The common theme threaded through the conversations always seemed to touch on two words: new community.

We began to form a board of directors. My vision attracted leaders such as Bob Curvin, who along with his Rutgers classmate and friend, William Payne, had organized Rutgers' first student chapter of the NAACP. Under Bob's leadership Newark's CORE chapter was aggressive when it came to racial-equality. Bob agreed to board the train that Curtis Mayfield was singing about. "People get ready, there's a train comin'/ You don't need no baggage, you just get on board."

Then there was Timothy Still. He worked nights at Budweiser and was in charge of all the tenant associations for the city's public housing. He was a reliable person to have in the trenches of this new adventure. Tim was appointed vice president of the first board of directors of New Community. Elma Bateman, also a parishioner at Queen of Angels, was appointed board secretary and played an important role in the development of a cultural arts component for our proposed new community. Her keen theatrical interest attracted the likes of playwright and actor, Vinnette Carroll, to New Community productions. Joe pledged his board membership, along with Monsignor Carey, with their focus set on addressing the needs of the people. When I first arrived at Queen of Angels in 1963, Arthur Bray was someone I befriended, who also happened to be the director of the Essex County Planning Board. His allegiance to the board was accompanied with a wealth of expertise for our cause. And Kenneth Gibson, who was then a chief engineer for the Newark Housing Authority, also agreed to serve on the board.

Willie Wright, a parishioner at Queen of Angels, was as outlandish as they come. He was tall, dark and lean and sported a mean goatee and rarely followed protocol. But every organization needs a Willie, because he had a unique way of making things happen. As a group, we decided that Willie should be board president. As a bunch of young mavericks, we held onto not much else than our hopes, dreams and ideas for a better tomorrow. With Willie as the conductor (heaven help us all), I was grateful God was on board with us as well.

As one of the founding board members of what would become New Community Corporation, my role first and foremost was to spread God's love. And considering the hopeless condition of the Central Ward, we used any means necessary in our strategic plan to sow and nurture what was desperately missing: hope. We were aligned with something bigger than ourselves. And although we didn't always agree on everything, the one thing that we did agree on was our commitment and vision for the long haul. And it was from that place, out of the ashes came hope. We banded together as a group with three goals in mind:

1. To develop safe, sound attractive housing for low income residents, depending on a community of people sharing and caring for one another as a new community for the Central Ward.

2. To promote interest, pride and responsibility through community participation in the housing development process. Local residents would be encouraged to participate actively in the design process.

3. To use new housing development to spur the revitalization of the Central Ward.

We also created our guiding mission statement: "To help residents of inner cities improve the quality of their lives to reflect individual God-given dignity and personal achievement." With our mission in place, we were ready to take this ride together. However, when the train left the station this time and with the proper signals in working order, all the right connections were made. Next stop: New Community Corporation.

CHAPTER 4

Manhattan College and The Immaculate Conception Seminary

When you look for me, you will find me. Yes, when you seek me with all your heart, I will let you find me – oracle of the Lord – and I will change your lot - Jeremiah 29:13-14

My father never finished school. However, he showed that he valued education by enrolling himself in classes such as a technical correspondence course. The courses were akin to an adult taking a class at the local community college, except the books and assignments arrived via mail. In addition to my father, my older sister, Ruth, attended Berkeley Business School and trained in secretarial work. Though college wasn't something that my family frequently discussed, it was quietly understood that I would attend one. Manhattan College was my first choice. As a kid, I listened to the track meets and basketball games broadcast over the radio and admired the school's teams. Also, my sister's husband, Robert Rohrman, was a graduate of Manhattan College. The school was familiar enough and close to home.

In 1954, I enrolled in Manhattan College to study engineering. It was there that my existing interest in the writings of Dorothy Day piqued. The *Catholic Worker* newspaper that she started had evolved into a movement. She was a devout Catholic who was also considered a radical. Day's strong belief in transforming people, building community and being of service to the poor and marginalized had a profound impact on me. I was experiencing what she had described in her writings as "a revolution of the heart."

My love of math and the sciences had led me to engineering, but my heart began to lead me in a different direction. My father had envisioned me being a public figure working in some area of government. However, my idea of public service would be much different than what my father had imagined. At age 18, while attending Manhattan College, I researched information on attending the seminary. I typically conferred with my father about things like this, but this wasn't one. I was torn between being an engineer or a follower of Jesus Christ. Certainly, it was not impossible for me to be an engineer and serve God at the same time. But dedicating my life to God to serve people by spreading Jesus' teachings would require my full attention.

My father always helped people in need. He was a very compassionate man and had set the tone for me. Yet, the conversation I had with my mother and father about me becoming a priest, was much harder for them to accept than I had anticipated. As I remember, he really didn't say much. Dad wanted a more prestigious life for me than his. He was a very proud man and I never wanted to disappoint him. He wanted both my sister and me to have a family. My sister was already married and they had two children of their own, Robert and Richard. But I believed with firm conviction that my calling lay elsewhere.

Besides my parents, there was still another person I was obligated to make a confession to about my love for God. Her name was Arlene and she was my prom date and had even been crowned in a beauty pageant as "Miss New York News." Arlene and I had grown very close. As it turned out, she wanted to date other people and I was intent on going forward with my relationship with God, so we eventually broke up. However, over the years, Arlene and I have managed to stay in contact with one another and make time to see each other at least once a year. The friendship superseded and survived my calling to be a priest.

Dad was allowing me to be my own man with my decision to go into the priesthood. After all, his life had meant so much to mine. In 1955, as I was halfway through my freshman year, my father, the anchor in my life, died suddenly. He was 53 years old. Despite what I was feeling about entering into the priesthood, my first responsibility was to the family.

I finished out that last semester at Manhattan College and because college credits at that time were not transferable, I sacrificed about 45 credits. However, Professor Amandus Leo, an influential dean of engineering at Manhattan College, stepped in. He was someone I looked up to. He was good friends with Robert Moses, chief engineer of the Brooklyn and Tappan Zee bridges, as well as the Port Authority building and other landmarks. Professor Leo made it so that my name was left on the rolls as an honorary student of the Manhattan School of Engineering while I would go into the seminary. So all was not lost considering that my engineering skills would serve me well later.

In the meantime, family came first and foremost with the sudden death of my father. I spent the next two academic years, from 1956 to 1957, at Seton Hall University studying classical language and philosophy, before going to the seminary. This worked out well for my family because my mother, who had taken it very hard when I announced that I was going into the priesthood, would still have me around. Campus life at that time held little interest to me, so living at home and being able to help my mother through the difficult loss of my father was where I needed to be. Had I pursued foreign missionary work, like I had once dreamt of, she would have suffered two losses – her husband and her son and Newark wouldn't have been a thought. Following God's Holy ordinance was the path that felt right to me.

In the fall of 1958 when I entered the Immaculate Conception Seminary in Darlington, New Jersey, my freedom to come and go as I pleased came to a screeching halt. This seminary served Hudson, Essex, Union and Bergen counties, which were under the auspices of an urban diocese, although the remote location of the seminary didn't suggest anything urban to me. This place was like being put out to pasture in rural America. With the exception of newspapers, a selection of magazines and the evening news on television, the outside world was largely cut off.

I spent the next six years of my life in the seminary. I went to class full time Monday through Friday and a half-day on Saturday. I quickly learned that you hardly ever had time for yourself. And the food was awful. You had to have an iron stomach and some people actually left the seminary due to the less than satisfactory food. Since my summers belonged to the seminary, I spent time during breaks working as a teacher at Boys Town, which was a reform school in Kearny, New Jersey. The faculty at the seminary was highly qualified, holding doctorate degrees from some of the most prestigious institutions in Europe. Yet, I couldn't help but feel as if I were in prison because of how the place was operated. In retrospect, surviving the seminary was a good thing because what was up the road for me was more than a mouthful of bad food.

During this time, my mother had become very independent. She had gotten her license and learned how to drive. She taught herself to type and was hired as a customer service representative for McGraw-Hill, the book publishing company. In a matter of a few years, she had accomplished quite a lot. I was comforted by the realization that the both of us had gotten on with our lives.

Back at the seminary, the amount of work and material that we were expected to cover was unlike anything I had ever endured. For one sociology project on race issues, I teamed up with a fellow classmate. The project gave my classmate and I the freedom to venture outside the seminary compound to do research. What had once served as mere classroom discussion, now involved taking a more microscopic look at the Black experience in America. I was discovering what the social terrain for black people in this country was really like.

During the mid to late '50s, the Civil Rights Movement started to heat up in the wake of the death of young Emmett Till on August 28, 1955. His savage killing sounded an alarm that created a collective consciousness among Black people. Whites even agreed that Jim Crow had to go. The oppressive treatment that black people endured really started to eat at me. It harkened me back to the time when my uncles were fighting in the war and even though I was just a kid, I had felt compelled to do something. At the seminary, my classmate and I wrote letters to national black organizations like the NAACP to set up interviews to access the information we needed for the research project

Prior to the research project, I'd had little contact with Black America. I can still remember my father telling me as a kid that a black family had moved into our working class neighborhood of West New York. It was a revelation, because there were no black people living in our community. Some people made a fuss about the family moving in. But the monsignor at the church where we attended, who seemingly had more clout than the mayor, put an immediate end to the squawking. "There'll be none of that," he said during Sunday Mass. "They have the right to live where they want to live," he told us. Before the seminary, I probably had been in the company of only one black person ever. I remembered him from a summer construction job. Even at the seminary Blacks were rare. There were just a few at the seminary studying to be priests. There was another black person I interacted with on a supply set-up for maintenance at the seminary. That was it. Yet, the plight of black people in America, as the focus of my research project, eventually became a real concern of mine.

While I made it through the seminary successfully, the powers that be wanted me to continue my education by working toward a doctorate degree in math, although I wanted absolutely no part of teaching at the time. I really didn't know what I was going to do, because there was no discussion about a church assignment for me.

Still dangling between the real world and purgatory, I was ordained as a priest on Saturday, May 25, 1963. Usually a newly ordained priest says his first Mass at his parish church, mine being St. Joseph's. My sister was living in Pennsylvania and I knew her pastor, Father John Healey, so I opted to say mine at my sister's church, Nativity of the Lord. Father Healey was delighted that I would say my first Mass there. It was beautiful. My mother and all her family attended along with my Aunt Rosemary, Aunt Agnes and Uncle Jack and Uncle Ray. I remember all the women were wearing large hats. And my mother and sister were dressed for the occasion in mink stoles. My mother was a sharp dresser, a class act. By now my sister Ruth and her husband Bob had five children, Robert, Richard, William, James and Marianne. My sister was also pregnant with their last child, Paul. Father Joseph Fitzpatrick, who would later become my mentor, was also there. I savored the occasion.

And with great irony I must mention that on that same day, 32 independent African nations formed the Organization of African Unity.

The year 1963 seemed to serve as a global amalgamation of black people. That Tuesday, I reported to the chancery in Newark, where the archbishop handed me an envelope with my assignment. This envelope held my future. All that I had imagined myself doing – serving God and His people – waited for me inside the envelope. I went outside and then opened it. While sliding my finger beneath the seal, I said this quick prayer: "God use me where I am most needed." To my surprise I was assigned to Queen of Angels Church in Newark, New Jersey, an all-black parish. I knew some of the priests who were there and it was considered a very progressive church. Priests were handpicked to go there. And as it turned out, I was chosen because of the sociology research project I'd done on race with my classmate that we later presented to the entire seminary. The professor of the course had given my name to Monsignor Carey, the former procurator administrator at the seminary, when I first got there. He had since moved on to become the administrative priest at Queen of Angels.

Despite my very limited interaction with the black community, I went to Newark with great anticipation. Everyone did not have access to freedom, justice and equality. The hypocrisy that seemed to exist in America was becoming quite visible to me. While caught in a maelstrom of social and political upheaval around the country, I found myself standing at the crossroads of a changing America. My journey to Newark would cause me to defiantly question my Catholic faith. God in heaven and of the universe had ordered my steps into a thicket of unknown uncertainty, into the wilderness of a broken city, where all hope was shattered and dreams snuffed out. Newark was a place sorely in need of God's love. My challenge was to manifest His love through deed.

At age 27, I had never set foot in Newark until the day I received my pastoral assignment. I had no idea what to expect. But because I believed in God's Providence, it resonated in me that Queen of Angels was where I was supposed to be.

CHAPTER 5

Beyond Twenty Priests

*For one believes with the heart that God raised him from the
dead, you will be saved* -Romans 10:10

It was the summer of 1967 and Monsignor Tom Carey, now the administrative priest at Queen of Angels, sent an SOS message to the Newark
Roman Catholic Archbishop Thomas Boland. The message stated: *You
ought to be here as moral support to your parishes that are staying here. No
one's leaving. But you ought to show your support. It might even be good if
you moved in for a couple of days into one of the rectories.* When a response
never came, it crystallized in my mind that the parish was, indeed,
being ignored. All the priests at Queen of Angels had sent Archbishop
Thomas Boland a number of urgent messages during the six-day melee.
We expected something from the archbishop, perhaps a pastoral letter
addressing the entire diocese about the whole race issue. We didn't even
get that! It would have been a step in the right direction, considering
that Queen of Angels was an all-black parish with more than 2,500
parishioners. However, the archbishop didn't acknowledge or show up
as the leader of the church during a time of crisis like the '67 summer
uprising.

There were no food stores available. Everything had been destroyed. The church was feeding up to 3,000 people a day. People were
hurting. Queen of Angels purchased truckloads of staple items, such as
Spam and potatoes, to supplement what was being collected from the
generous food donations from people in and around Newark. In the
aftermath of all that had just taken place, the parishioners at Queen

of Angels were on the frontline making sure people were able to eat every day.

Seven days later, the archbishop responded. He decided to hold a press conference at the church. He really made a fool of himself, because he picked up what was being said in the white community. Rumors had circulated that the disturbance was born from a conspiracy of some outside organizers, which, basically, was the establishment's initial explanation for what had taken place. I always felt the diocese should have gone on record about the Summer Disorders. A moral position should have been taken. Sadly, that didn't happen.

The archbishop's lack of action only confirmed what I already thought: Queen of Angels was treated differently from suburban parishes. Soon after I arrived at Queen of Angels in 1963, it was apparent to me that the church needed to offer programming to help the community. The allocation of funds by the Newark Roman Catholic Archdiocese was quite limited in comparison to our counterpart white suburban parishes. Further, this treatment wasn't only happening at Queen of Angels, but there were other urban parishes treated with the same disregard from the archdiocese, such as Christ the King Church in Jersey City and St. Mary's in Plainfield, which was evolving into a black parish, along with others.

In solidarity, we formed a coalition dubbed as "Twenty Priests." On behalf of our black parishioners, we addressed the issues that affected our individual parishes, including key issues from unemployment to education and housing. The archdiocese did little to include the black community in the decision-making process specific to the community. For starters, if a new priest was being assigned to a predominantly black parish, the parishioners certainly should have some input about the person, particularly since there were no black priests in the urban parishes.

On behalf of the Twenty Priests, I drafted a 12-page formal letter and sent it to the archbishop, making our points clearly:

"We're not trying to deal with the participation of people in the suburban parishes. But we need to deal with the fact that we do not have black priests, and if we're not going to have black priests, we need to find a new way to get the participation of everybody in this process."

Eventually the complaints made by the "Twenty Priests" seeped out into the public and wound up in a number of newspapers. One such article written in the *Daily World* in 1969 read as follows:

> The official church's concept is to change the liturgy from Latin to English. The poor are cold, hungry, housed in rat traps, largely ignored by the affluent society, denied employment opportunities, denied legal and moral rights, and the official church responds by changing the direction of the altar.

Our letter apparently fell on deaf ears. And that's when we went on record in the *Newark Evening News* with this statement: "For a decade, the drama and urgency of desperate need of the inner city has been ignored by the official church in Newark. The official church is apathetic. It's a racist."

The "Twenty Priests" campaign for the poor and underserved attracted national and international attention when we held a press conference at Military Park Hotel on January 10, 1969. The letter we had written to the archbishop was distributed at the press conference. The Rev. Francis Schiller from Jersey City, along with Monsignor Carey and a number of other faithful servants of the Lord stood with me.

Our campaign reached as far as Holland, where Princess Beatrix heard about us. Soon thereafter, she visited New Jersey with her husband, Prince Claus, who was an environmental planner, at the request of my dear friend Paul Ylvisaker. At the time Ylvisaker was working closely with Governor Richard Hughes' Meadowlands Commission. Having heard about Twenty Priests, the princess requested to meet privately with me while she was in New Jersey. That chance meeting touched my soul and I was more than obliged to be in her company.

However, at the press conference, things were not quite as cordial. "You're nothing but a bunch of Communist Priests," shouted a woman named Catherine Crilly, who identified herself as a "good Catholic." She was quickly escorted out of the room by police. But why were we being labeled as Communist priests? Because we were trying to shed light on the blatant lack of concern for what was going on in urban churches? That's not to say the woman wasn't a good Catholic. Rather, it was her ideological conditioning as a white Catholic American that had limited her from seeing through the barrier of race that kept us separated from one another.

The next day's headline in the *Daily World* read, "Newark priests urge Church expel racism." Obviously, that didn't go over well with the Newark Roman Catholic Archdiocese administration. Then there was the article that ran in the *New York Times* where I was quoted as saying, "They were very much racist and they still are if you define racism as not allowing black and Spanish-speaking people to project themselves into leadership positions in the Archdiocese." What was now front and center made me reflect back on the experience the newly formed NCC Board of Directors had with the Mount Carmel Guild, an offshoot of the archdiocese. When we tried to get black leadership on their housing board, only to have them flat out rejected for no explainable reason, the racism in the Catholic Church could no longer be denied.

The Roman Catholic Church, which I loved and was tied to serve as one of its missionaries, had been flipped upside down. The Twenty Priests advised the archbishop that he should appoint a black advisory council. He needed to hear from the people, but, sadly, he refused to listen. Nothing seemed to make sense. I'd chosen to follow Jesus' teachings and here I was rebuking the authority of the Catholic Church, although I felt very strongly about what I was doing by calling the Church out on its racist practices. I, too, understood that Jesus was a pretty radical guy back in his day. It was all about forging a better path toward brotherhood. At least that's what I thought I was signing up for when I made the decision to become a priest. This experience tested my faith in the Church in ways that I never thought possible.

Willie Wright, who was already labeled a militant, got a kick out of me, because I was always getting in trouble with the archdiocese. Willie was also the president of the United Black Catholics and supported my lead to expose the Church. My involvement with Twenty Priests was just the start of my woes with the Church.

The black men from Queen of Angels, such as Willie, were a

prayerful group of leaders. They were trying to share their ministries with the diocese, but the Church wasn't hearing them. In the Bible, men fasted in order to focus their attention on God's work. They wanted education, housing and employment ministries. Willie and others followed that lead. I recall the men at the church not eating for nearly two weeks at one time. Their presence was really visible at the church with all the physical work they did. Indeed, they were servants of the Lord and of the community.

The truth of the matter was that being black and Catholic was not a popular choice. In his role as board president of New Community, Willie had once arranged a meeting with the archbishop that included two fellow board members, Arthur Bray and Joe, and New Community attorney, Irvin Booker. The purpose of the meeting was to request $200,000 from the Newark Roman Catholic Archdiocese for our proposed "new community" housing development project. When the archdiocese denied his request, Willie was game for whatever dust I was kicking up.

Although Black Catholics were a growing population in the 1970s, many of them from Queen of Angels parish attended 8 a.m. Mass, because they didn't want to be ridiculed by their own people for attending a Catholic church. In our effort to expose the Church, we refused to let up on our mission to see to it that black people were included in an equal opportunity Catholic experience. During this time and approaching Good Friday, 150 black parishioners from Queen of Angels planned a march on Sacred Heart Cathedral in Newark. When the cathedral got wind that we were coming, they cancelled their Good Friday services. This march was an important statement made by this group of Black Catholics. Carrying a large cross, Joe Chaneyfield led the march, accompanied by myself and several other white priests.

"Agitate."

"Agitate."

"Agitate."

Within me the spirit of Frederick Douglass was alive and well. We even picketed in front of the archbishop's residence. He would always hold that against me.

In 1973, I was abruptly removed from my beloved Queen of Angels after 10 years of service. I was exiled to a dormant St. Joseph Parish in Newark, where Richard McGinness was the administrative priest. I was essentially told that I would not get another church home. Was the Church really trying to oust me? It didn't matter because I took my punishment in stride, although there were times when I felt anxiety over the situation. I was made to feel like an outcast.

I was grateful for my studies at Fordham University, where I was continuing to work toward my graduate degree in Sociology. Hitting the books kept my mind from wandering into the abyss of "what if's." I was also thankful for the guidance of my mentor, Father Joseph Fitzpatrick, the renowned scholar, Jesuit, activist and sociologist, during this time.

In the 1950s, Father Fitzpatrick rattled the Church and the white population for their contempt and hostility toward the new migration of Puerto Ricans into New York. He insisted that tolerance and respect be shown to Puerto Ricans and that the Church be amenable to the cultural needs of the community. With his guidance, I refused to buckle under the pressure, some two decades after his grand stand.

During this laissez-faire time in my life, I traveled to Rome, Italy, home of the Roman Catholic Church. It was here that I came face to face with myself, my God, and my Church. Had my radical ideas and ways gone too far? Had I pushed the envelope further than I should have? I was searching for answers to help reconcile my spiritual belief that God does not make mistakes that my actions were in good faith and in honor of my Lord and Savior, Jesus Christ.

My soul and I felt estranged. Feeling empty, I wandered throughout the city, lost in more ways than one. I visited St. Peter's Basilica, which could have swallowed Queen of Angels whole, more than twice, with plenty of room to spare. The omnipotence of the structure was beyond comparison. While Michelangelo's larger than life "Pieta," a marble rendering of the Virgin Mary holding the dead body of Christ, was a soothing elixir for my somber spirit. After all, Jesus had died so that I could have eternal life. I was reminded by this flawless sculpture to get on with my work. The exquisite gardens around the city and fountains were as refreshing as they were meditative. The more places I visited, the more the Balm of Gilead befriended me. Spiritually revived by the evidence of God's presence, I was starting to feel like myself again.

As it turned out, an actual case had been brought against me at the Vatican. A detailed report about my pastoral side was on file, and I just happened to meet some of the priests who were on the panel that reviewed my case. When they learned that more adult baptisms were performed at Queen of Angels than at any other parish in the Newark Roman Catholic Archdiocese, the panel of priests pretty much closed my case.

Not long thereafter, Boland resigned and with his resignation, Peter Gerety was assigned as the new archbishop of the Newark Roman Catholic Archdiocese. He had spent close to 20 years at a black and Hispanic parish in New Haven, Connecticut, and clearly understood the situation going on in Newark.

In 1974, I was reassigned to St. Rose of Lima Parish in the Roseville section of Newark, where I became its pastor in 1977. A year later, the Rev. Joseph A. Francis, a black man, became one of four black Roman Catholic bishops in the country. He served Newark for 19 years speaking out against racism.

I am convinced that Archbishop Gerety's recommendation to Pope John Paul II that I receive the rank of "Prelate of Honor," a distinction that rendered me the title of "Reverend Monsignor" in 1986, had everything to do with his effort to protect me. I was grateful for the extra breathing space and God's good grace.

MONSIGNOR WILLIAM J. LINDER

CHAPTER 6

Road Trip

Complete my joy by being of the same mind, with the same love, united in heart, thinking one thing – Philippians 2:2

The future tenants of New Community Homes Court needed a real visual of the finished product of what we were hoping to build. It was also important for the proposed tenants to see a black man like Roger Glasgow, who NCC hired as the chief architect for the project to build New Community's first housing complex for working class families in Newark. Glasgow arranged for us to take a weekend bus trip to Columbia, Maryland, and Reston, Virginia, to see the planned "New Model Cities." It was my friend, Paul Ylvisaker, who helped implement President Lyndon Johnson's "model-cities" national program, as an urban planner that included the cities of Columbia and Reston.

Arthur Bray proved to be a valuable asset on these outings, because he made it possible for us to have access to local planning officials, in his respective position as director of planning for Essex County. The coordinated presentations lent more credence to what we were doing and further substantiated tenant input. The beauty in our effort was the absence of a hierarchy. We were all in this together as one unit.

On another outing, the group went to New York to see a housing project called "The Harlem Triangle," which had a reputation for good tenant leadership. We also visited some townhouses in Philadelphia that were part of their center-city development. Since urban neighborhoods were our focus, it was important that we see the possibilities of what the Central Ward of Newark could look like. Promoting leadership was important to us. And though Reston and Columbia were planned cities and not urban communities, they still afforded us with the experience of learning from all aspects of how to put *our* new community altogether.

As the planning process moved forward, we realized that just because we had established a black-controlled board of directors that did not automatically mean, the people in the community would always be included in the decision-making process. The people on the board had the final decision-making power. Therefore, we created the New Community Advisory Council to work in conjunction with the board of directors.

In every step of the process, we made headway by giving more responsibility to our prospective tenants, further underscoring the principle of self-sufficiency. The community advisory council would have authority in a number of areas that pertained to the development of housing. For example, the plans submitted to the state for housing were developed and approved by the advisory council.

The preliminary projections of the 45-acre land designated for New Community were drawn up by Art and his county planning aides. An article that ran in the *Newark Evening News* on February 29, 1968, quoted Art saying, "I don't know of anything in the United States to equal it. We will be building a new community within an old community. People (from the community) will operate it just the same as they would operate any small town; it will be their community."

Tim Still, vice president of NCC, chimed in confirming what Art had said. "It's a beautiful plan and the important thing is that we're going to run the corporation," Tim said.

But even with the strong leadership and support for the project, there's no doubt that people thought we were out of our minds with our proposal. We needed to take action. The community was so used to being told what to do as opposed to having a well- thought out strategic plan. My role was to get them to believe what they could do, and I was willing to suffer whatever consequences came my way. Building a "new community" was revolutionary. The founding board members of NCC, as New Community Corporation came to be called in shorthand, were the revolutionaries.

It was my job as a religious leader to empower the community to believe and to restore a sense of hope that, indeed, we could build a new community. In spite of everything Newark had been through, faith and hope sustained our efforts to rebuild the city's Central Ward.

In the past, Blacks in the community who had raised their voices in opposition of the status quo were usually bought off with a job that paid much more than what they were earning. The coalition that we were building was resistant to that kind of crookedness. The principle of self-sufficiency had been activated and it was all the motivation the people needed in the Central Ward to take control of their community.

CHAPTER 7

Growing up Linder

Happy is the man who cares for the poor and the weak – Psalm 41:1

All of who I am has everything to do with my first teachers: my parents. I was blessed to have grown up in a household with a compassionate father and mother whose love of God fueled me to spend 50 years in the priesthood. My mother spent part of each day in prayer. I continued this tradition by saying Mass every day for the last 50 years. They laid the foundation.

My folks didn't have much money in the bank and amassing wealth wasn't a priority. Dad either spent his money on the family, or gave it away to charity. My parents set a very high standard for what it meant to serve others.

Growing up in the Linder household in West New York, New Jersey, was never dull because Dad was also a fun guy. I had such admiration and respect for him because he was a very interesting person, from his being the helpful next door neighbor to his political involvement. I remember one particular time when a neighbor of ours was having trouble with an electrical outlet. Dad worked for the Public Service Electric Company in Hudson County, but for some reason, he sent me over to the neighbor's house to assess the situation. I couldn't have been more than 12 years old at the time. The surprised look on the neighbor's face when I showed up at their front door said it all.

"Billy what can I do for you today?" asked Mrs. Harris.

"My Dad sent me over to fix your electrical outlet," I responded, armed with a toolbox. Mrs. Harris' eyebrows arched, as if thinking: *You have got to be kidding me.* With some trepidation, she escorted me into the room with the problem outlet. I went to work. To her surprise, I fixed and replaced the outlet. Dad had passed on his knowledge of electrical distribution and most matters pertaining to electricity to me. I was like his little apprentice.

If my Dad thought I was capable of doing something, he didn't hold me back. Our one-on-one time together usually was spent with my father showing me how to fix or build something. He dabbled in photography, as a hobby, and would give me pointers on how to take good photos and develop them. He was his own carpenter, plumber and auto mechanic. Self-sufficiency was his philosophy. Therefore, he was adamant about me being independent. We shared a very close father and son relationship. After all, I was somewhat his namesake. He was William Frederick Linder and I was born William Joseph Linder on June 5, 1936, at Christ Hospital, in Jersey City, during the Great Depression. My middle name was a small distinction that kept me from being referred to as junior.

I looked a lot like my father physically as well. He was an average height man about 5'10 and kept himself in pretty good physical shape. His German background emphasized strong values, chiefly the importance of family. He was always instructing me about my obligations to my mother and sister Ruth, who was almost ten years older than me. Ruth was raised to stay very close to the family and was more sheltered. By the time I came along as the new addition to the family, she was good and spoiled. From the start, my father prepared me to take the lead. I believe this had everything to do with him having to quit school at the age of 13 to work in the family's bakery business, after his father died.

My mother, Madeleine, had come from a large family of nine, and was of German and Irish descent. Her maiden name was Eibell, which came from her German side. On the Irish side was her mother, whose family name was Harrigan. The Irish traits prevailed in our household and my mother's side of the family was a fun bunch to be around.

Ray and Rich were my mother's brothers and they owned a painting business. They'd swing by whenever they were in our neighborhood and picked me up to help them with a job. I spent many summers working for them. By the time I was in high school, they would send me out to check on various job sites to make sure the work was of the highest quality and ready for inspection. They taught me at a young age how to handle a paintbrush like a pro, how to cut edges with a brush and how to master painting window panes and sills. That was a real skill. In general, I learned the difference between shoddy work and good workmanship. Since Mom was the oldest of her siblings and my grandparents on both sides had all died by the time I was five years old, all my uncles looked up to her and my father as parental figures.

My childhood seemed fairly peaceful until my uncles had to go and fight in World War II. Saying goodbye to them wasn't easy. My uncles had done everything with me. They were a major part of my eight-year-old world. I struggled to make sense of it all. War. With war came blackouts and the blaring siren signaling that all the lights in the house were to be turned off, shades pulled down and curtains drawn. In the still of night and total darkness, it amplified in my mind the understanding that war was a serious matter. We waited nervously for the alarm to sound so we could return to normal. All the while hearing conversations that German U-boat submarines were stationed out in the Hudson River, just twenty minutes away from where we lived. Hearing about the eminent threat of German airstrikes was unnerving. These blackouts were to protect us from the enemy seeing the greater New York area as a potential target. That meant my uncles, who were overseas actually fighting *in* the war, were in real danger. It became crystal clear to me that I might not ever see them again. The most frightening thing I could have ever imagined was that they could become casualties of war.

Trying to reconcile the paradox of love and war and the possible loss of my beloved uncles ignited a sense of urgency in me to make the situation better. That foundational desire has never left me. As an eight-year-old child, I came to understand that life was tenuous and fragile and not to be taken for granted. In a calculated effort to help my uncles, I organized some classmates from St. Joseph's Grammar School, and other neighborhood kids to do a scrap metal drive. It seems almost comical now, but at the time I was on a serious mission. My uncles' lives were at stake. And metal was a valuable commodity that could be recycled and used to produce war goods that could possibly procure their safety. My squadron wore matching armbands, and we probably looked more like Spanky McFarland and his gang of "Little Rascals" than anything else.

Nevertheless, my father championed our cause. "Just leave it out in front of the house," he said. "And when I come home from work I'll get it to the right place." By the time he got home, we had collected a pretty big pile. It took up two parking spaces. Our hard work and community service had paid off. There I was on the front page of the newspaper, along with my squadron, merely for having helped out in the war effort. It had seemed to me like the right thing to do. I remember feeling proud, in the flash of the moment, as the photographer snapped the picture. What I learned from the experience was that hard work was nothing to be afraid of because it had its just reward. More importantly, my uncles' eventual safe return home meant everything was returning back to normal.

My father enjoyed taking our family on vacations and we would often visit with my mother's aunt and uncle who lived in Saratoga, New York. They had a big, sprawling home on ten acres of land. During the summer, we'd spend a week or two there. Mom's Aunt Agnes, who was a chiropractor, was a pioneer in the field of medicine. She was really feisty and had been arrested on more than one occasion, because back then they would arrest chiropractors for impersonating doctors. Aunt Agnes used to crack me up with stories about how she stood up to the cops while in handcuffs. She also had these little sayings that were fun to ponder.

"Billy boy," she would say, while squeezing my cheeks to make her point, "you get nothing out of life being scared." With vivid imagery and a quirky sense of humor, she fostered in me early on a sense of resolve and fearlessness. "Or you'll wind up sleeping on a bed of nails and unhappy for the rest of your days," she quipped. Well, I didn't want to sleep on a bed of nails for the rest of my life so I chose to be brave, no matter what.

Once a month, as part of my education, Dad would take the family out to eat. Although his choice of food was limited, he didn't limit

MONSIGNOR WILLIAM J. LINDER

mine and introduced me to foods other than what he enjoyed. It was important to him for me to be well-rounded and able to fit in anywhere. Food was a great starting point for a growing boy, as it opened up my appreciation for different cultures.

My mother was a housewife but also worked part-time at a millinery shop. Back then a woman wasn't considered well-dressed if she wasn't wearing a hat. I am sure that's where my mother met many of her friends. Along with my father, she was very involved in our church, St. Joseph's of the Palisades. I would describe my mother as being socially connected.

The Jewish population was well represented in North Hudson County. And my mother was friends with an older Jewish woman who also had a son. When the woman's son joined the military and later went off to dental school, my mother loaned me out as a surrogate son, so to speak, to this woman. I would check in with her to see if she needed anything and to make sure things were okay.

In our neighborhood, people looked after one another. It was a real community. The city was invested in its youth. The city's council members were involved with the children in the community. They coached various youth sports leagues. One of the council members actually ran a day camp that didn't cost us anything. They organized weekend camping trips. And during the summer, posted on the wall down at City Hall, was the Yankees' baseball schedule. The only thing we had to do was sign up, show up and get on the bus, which was driven by one of the council members to the games. This was all free. Even our mayor was very active in the Boys Scout troop that I belonged to.

The one thing missing in North Hudson, as far as recreational activities, was a swimming pool. That's why the Catholic Youth Organization (CYO) in Jersey City became a favorite place of mine, because it had a pool. Another favorite hangout of mine was the basketball court. One day while playing basketball, I got a bad gash on my lip and tongue that required stitches. My mother, who supported my father's idea of me being independent, called the doctor's office and told him I was on my way. There was no formal escort to the doctor's office with my mother holding my hand. I went alone, bloody mouth and all.

I was being shaped by many of my experiences: growing up in a stable home environment, dealing with my feelings of war. I lived in a loving community where people kept tabs on one another. My mother would engage in conversation with neighbors at the local A & P supermarket, and Dad was the helpful handyman next door. We ate out once a month and vacationed once a year. My world was an idyllic setting like the television show "Father Knows Best."

However, the four years I spent at St. Peter's Preparatory High School in Jersey City caused some discoloration in the rose-colored glasses through which I had been viewing the world. My father and I agreed that St. Peter's Prep, was the right place for me, as opposed to St. Joseph's, the parish high school, where my sister had attended. The Jesuit priests at St. Peter's Prep had a reputation and, according to my father, they could teach a rock to learn. Not that I was a bad student, but they really kept me focused and dealt sternly with my stubbornness.

My high school interests varied from running track to working on the literary magazine. However, butting heads with Father Thomas Murray during my freshman year was where I truly got schooled. Latin was a required four-year course at St. Peter's. *Is this guy for real*, I thought, when Father Murray started assigning all the required work for his class. When in this life will I ever need Latin? That was my attitude. It made absolutely no sense to me whatsoever that I should have to take it. So I squandered away two marking periods of Father Murray's class and failed the course twice.

"My class seems to be something of a joke to you William," Father Murray soberly said one day. "Either you're not too bright, which I don't believe, or you're living in a world of fantasy if you think I am going to pass you. May God bless you my son."

God bless me ... It's not like I'm going to be a priest, was my smart aleck thought that I dare not say out loud because I knew better. As it turned out, Father Murray was more determined than I was stubborn. I racked up enough detention that had he sent me to the detention room, called the "jug," I would have been expelled from school. Instead, Father Murray protected me, having me serve my punishment under his supervision.

That meant I spent all of my Christmas and Easter vacation and mostly every Saturday in detention with Father Murray, in his classroom. I grew impressed by Father Murray's commitment to teach me. Despite having failed Latin twice, I received an honor pin because of my overall high aptitude in my other courses. The fact that Father Murray did not give up on me, sparked me to pass Latin for the next four marking periods of my freshman year and every year thereafter. Father Murray really cared and his dedication stuck with me. It's much easier to give up on people and toss them aside. I learned from Father Murray that people matter. I mattered.

Another lesson that I learned while attending St. Peter's came from a dictum that the Jesuit priests preached: God does not exclude or discriminate. Labeled "God's Marines," the Jesuits' armament of strong moral conviction included embracing education and social justice for all people. They were known as the "Society of Jesus." They possessed the intelligence of academics and encouraged their charges to rise as critical thinkers. The Jesuit brothers, particularly those in South America, believed in Liberation Theology. They were the voice for the voiceless and the Jesuits' wild compassion for the poor held the Catholic faith accountable to the societal ill of poverty. During the 1980s, some Jesuits' belief in Liberation Theology was labeled too radical by the Vatican in Rome, and as a result Liberation Theology was frowned upon.

The Jesuits practiced mental calisthenics when it came to challenging me to think righteously. I was also influenced by my weekly readings of *The Catholic Worker* newspaper, written by Dorothy Day. In class, topics like the unanimous decision by the Supreme Court to overturn "separate but equal," in the case of *Brown vs. the Board of Education,* were central to some of our classroom discussions. As part of the Brown case, there was a simple exercise conducted by psychologist Kenneth Clark that revealed how black children thought of themselves. Black children picked the white doll as the prettiest and smartest over the black doll. I was shocked that "inferiority" had already marred their existence. It was permanently stamped into these children's psyches that they were less than white children. Based on my studies, black children were doomed from the start. This was a defining moment for me, because up until then I'd never given race much thought. My life experiences said something otherwise but it was this "race" thing that kept gnawing at me in high school. Years later, I would meet Dr. Kenneth Clark, who I had the honor of having dinner with when he was conducting a study on the racial policies at UMDNJ, at the request of New Jersey Governor Thomas Kean.

I began to see race as a societal plague engineered by a supremacist Eurocentric view and wholly contrary to God's holy order. Being in the grasp of the Jesuits, who were religious social warriors, helped in sharpening my ideas to a keen point. The Jesuits taught me that being born of one color or another was God given! This racial hierarchy predicated on skin color was a man-made perception - that had nothing to do with God. By and large, my experience had been that white people believed in God and practiced their faith. But for them to claim racial superiority, when it was now my belief that God created all men the same, was egotistical lunacy.

The Jesuit's focus on missionary work profoundly touches me. They were globally connected to foreign lands long before globalization became the catchphrase of the day. The Jesuit brothers ingrained the concepts of social justice with the ferocity of an army platoon sergeant who drills his troops. I knew because I was a part of the Reserve Officers Training Corp (ROTC) program. That experience played an important role in shaping my worldview.

As a teen in high school, the stirrings of civil rights and equality for black people showed up as a blip on my heart's radar. Hanging out with my friends in New York City was a favorite pastime of mine and I worked at the A&P to keep money in my pockets for a fun time in the city. While mingling at Jones Beach for a concert or traipsing through the city, I began to meet people with different backgrounds. I also began to question the status quo around me. Why were the lives of black people so much different from mine? That question became increasingly vexing. In my reality of West New York, New Jersey, black people simply weren't visible and thus they didn't exist. Seeing life as I had through rose-colored glasses was no longer an option. During my senior year in high school, and much to my surprise, I seriously started to consider serving God as a vocation.

CHAPTER 8

And a Child Shall Lead: Queen of Angels Youth Movement

*Train the young in the way they should go; even when old,
they will not swerve from it* – Proverbs 22:6

Queen of Angels Church became a family compound and there was nothing that couldn't be solved at the parish. The people never felt isolated or alienated at Queen of Angels. Everyone belonged. It was also a great resource for housing and employment information. The church established a free medical clinic, with services provided by Dr. Leon Smith, who was associated with St. Michael's Hospital, and parishioner Eunice Graham, who was also a nurse. Dr. Smith served the poor and their children with the same compassion as he did for his affluent patients who had the resources to pay him.

The church was expanding as an advocate for the community. When Father Thomas Comerford came to Queen of Angels a few years after I started, his arrival sparked national attention at the church. He led the tenants of the Stella Wright Homes on a two-year rent strike from 1970 to 1972, one of the longest in the nation. By the time the strike ended, many of the tenants had saved enough money to purchase their own homes, because Father Comerford had opened a bank account for the striking tenants to deposit their rent money. He ultimately wound up serving time in jail for his actions. But I'd say it was well worth the 30 days or so that he spent at the county jail for all those who were able to become homeowners.

The church was literally running out of space because it was quickly becoming the social hub of the community. We eventually had to rent an apartment at one of the public housing buildings to hold our prayer meeting service. The parish then rented two storefront properties - one dealt with housing complaints and the other handled summer programs for the youth. We had a vibrant group of young people, including Willie Wright's four children and Joe Chaneyfield's daughters: Rosemary, Peggy, Joanne and Gayle. We trained them, along with others at the church, through programs such as the "Young Christian Students," which consisted of three different age groups, and the "Young Christian Workers," a group of post-high school graduates, some of whom were attending college. Our efforts were modeled after a system the French used after World War II to counter communism and it was very influential in bringing about meaningful change.

I worked with the Young Christian Workers, who acted as moderators and leaders for the high school students. There was always a scripture reading followed by discussion. Then the young people were taught to observe, judge and act, courtesy of the strategy used by the Young Christian Workers. Much of what I was teaching our youth was to be a part of something bigger than themselves. For change to really take place in Newark, it all had to start with the youth. I saw that for myself in the march from Selma to Montgomery, Alabama. Besides, the lesson I took away from the Kenneth Clark experiment with the black and white dolls, was a frightening revelation to me. That black children were psychologically imprinted with a permanent stamp of low self-esteem. I vowed that the youngsters at Queen of Angels would not fall victim to a similar fate of low self-perception. They knew I had certain expectations for them, and that I believed in them, just as Father Murray back at St. Peter's in Jersey City had believed in me in my most obstinate teenage moments. I believed that they all had the potential to do great things.

Barry Washington was a perfect example. An active member of our youth group, Washington grew up in the Hayes Homes public housing projects. Later in his adult life, he co-founded Connection Communications Corporation that first brought cable television to

Newark. It became the largest minority owned cable TV system in the nation. That kind of belief in oneself, no matter where you come from, coupled with their commitment to engage in a number of hours of religious studies, gave them a strong moral foundation. These weren't any willy-nilly kids. What better way for them to deal with the social complexities of their time than being directly involved in making some necessary changes. I cheered them on with enthusiasm, revving them up at every opportunity. I wanted them to know that they had the power and it was time to seize the moment.

However, in addition to keeping the youth busy, we gave them space to have fun and explore. They had the same kind of rambunctious energy I had as a teenager, going to parties and hanging out. They were all active in our Catholic Youth Organization. We made sure there was always something for them to do. Thanks to Governor Hughes, we received funding for recreational trips to take the kids down to the Jersey shore. While spending leisure time at the shore, the Governor noticed there were no kids of color having fun at the beach. He appealed to the legislature for recreational funding for inner-city youth. In return, the kids had a blast.

Then there were the festive parades that involved the kids, along with employment opportunities and their dances that kept the church jumping. The line to get into the dances would stretch all the way down the street. Many of the young people from the community were turned away, because there just wasn't enough room for them to get in. As a result, the dances helped the youth group at the church raise a lot of money. It had one of the largest bank accounts of all the other groups within the church.

Our efforts led the youth at Queen of Angels to become politically active. They eventually arrived at the realization that there was power in numbers and took on the city of Newark. They were fantastic. In 1964, our young people brought a lawsuit against Mayor Hugh Addonizio on the matter of substandard housing. For two years, the group researched case law, read newspapers, spoke to attorneys and diligently gathered all the legal background. Everything was dated; there were monthly housing inspections documented by the students and interviews conducted with families who lived in these rundown houses. They took pictures of the absolute horrid conditions at houses owned by slumlords. A faculty member at Rutgers Law School handled the lawsuit for us. The case exposed one slumlord and uncovered that he hadn't been paying his taxes. He went to jail for tax evasion. These young people were developing into real leaders and with the outcome of the lawsuit they had even more incentive to do more.

"Keep the pressure on" was the leadership motto our youth adopted at Queen of Angels. It was also a tactic used by Saul Alinsky, who is known today as the "Father of Community Organizing." He was someone I was a big fan of, because of his radical way of bringing attention to an issue and his compassion toward the underserved black population. The son of Russian immigrants, Alinsky was praised by Malcolm X for knowing more about community organizing than anyone else he knew.

Alinsky's approach to activism was very much alive in our youth. I realized what they were doing wasn't just an extracurricular activity: the youth were being molded into determined community activists. So at the church we gave them even more tools. A space that had once been a storage area was converted into a large classroom with a conference table and a bank of twelve telephones. The kids were active in calling people and getting them to come out to various rallies. They were real social networkers. A large city map was installed that went from the ceiling to the floor to assist them in honing in on their next target. With all the training they were receiving, it was now time for them to confront, as Alinsky said, "the enemy."

When Addonizio was hosting some of his old congressional buddies on the steps of City Hall - more for publicity than anything else -the kids went down to City Hall to confront him. They milled about innocently, in different groups, and then someone gave a signal and they all converged on him. Addonizio was caught off guard as they chanted: "Addonizio supports slumlords." Their concealed posters and signs were then raised in full display with images of dilapidated housing plastered on them. They totally humiliated Addonizio in front of his friends from Congress.

By then, Queen of Angels was the hub of social activity. With the young people deeply connected to what was politically happening, it offered a life-altering experience for them and the history of Newark. On March 27, 1968, Rev. Dr. Martin Luther King Jr., came to Newark to garner support for the "Poor People's" march and campaign he was planning to lead in Washington, D.C. on April 22, 1968.

Our youth were on the frontline when two field agents from the Southern Christian Leadership Conference, which was headed by Dr. King, were dispersed to Newark in advance of his arrival. They worked the bank of telephones with the agents to coordinate housing and hotel arrangements for those who would be traveling to the march. Joyce Smith Carter, an active member of Queen of Angels youth group, actually served as Dr. King's secretary during his stay.

Naturally, Dr. King's visit received a lot of media coverage. You could see it in the students' eyes how overwhelmed they were to be involved in something so important. Filled with a great sense of pride, these newly ordained activists were the backbone of changing times in Newark, just as I had witnessed with the young people in the march from Selma to Montgomery.

Dr. King's motorcade rode slowly through the Central Ward, in the aftermath of the '67 Summer Disorders, with the gravitas of a funeral procession. Yet the palpable buzz of spirited love and togetherness that emanated from the crowd seemed to suggest Dr. King's presence wasn't just some random visit. A sense of hope could be seen in the eyes of the young people as Dr. King's motorcade processed. As it turned out, Newark was Dr. King's last big-city stop before he embarked on his final destination to Memphis, Tennessee, where he was killed on April 4, 1968.

MONSIGNOR WILLIAM J. LINDER

CHAPTER 9

Operation Understanding and Operation Housewives

*Do not conform yourselves to this age but be transformed
by the renewal of your mind, that you may discern what
is the will of God, what is good, and pleasing and perfect*
– Romans 12:2

Queen of Angels was this enchanting place. We brought the community of 35,000 blacks and whites together for a march for understanding, after the July '67 Summer Disorders. In August of that year, following the nationally televised social upheaval, Joe Chaneyfield led the marchers through the "ghetto," as the Central Ward was called. Joe and Dave Foley, a managing partner with Arthur Young & Company accounting firm, were co-chairs of the march for understanding. And that was the genesis of "Operation Understanding." The march for understanding received a lot of press coverage. NCC made a commitment to rebuild the Central Ward - a nice sound bite for the media. I distinctly remember a white woman from Montclair that toured the area, saying to a reporter: "You never realize just how bad it is here until you examine it up close. It's incredibly bad."

White people from suburbia were still in the dark on the transformation happening in Newark. There was absolutely no understanding of how much black people had suffered in America. Understanding the subjugation of race and how it provoked and diminished the already tortured lives of the black community was worlds away from white suburbia. Was there any concern at all on their part? "Operation Understanding" was an up-close and informative approach to talking about race relations in the city. There was a more honest discourse about race back then than it is today. What we see now is President Obama, a black man who holds the highest office in the land, although America's societal infrastructure remains contingent upon race, which is perpetuated by police brutality and the inhumane number of Black Americans incarcerated. Operation Understanding offered an opportunity for white people to learn about the marginalization of the black community in Newark. They needed to understand that the pain was real. The same as it is today.

Queen of Angels was more than a parish. It was a spiritual force and progressive prescription for what was ailing the community. The '67 Summer Disorders had served as an ugly and unsightly blemish on the face of Newark. When it finally came to a head and burst, the unsightly puss spilled forth and now it was time to clean the mess up. The healing began with the two races coming together in a non-threatening manner through our work with Operation Understanding. That moment in time called for help in healing the social paralysis that had existed between the black and white races. We needed the entire community to come together.

Whenever the parishioners complained about something in the community, I would ask them: "So what are you going to do about it?" The greatest significance of the march was the statement it made. In essence, the black community was standing up and saying: "We're not going anywhere, so we need to figure this out – black and white people together."

The action assigned to Operation Understanding drew white and black people together to form teams – a black urban resident along with a white suburban resident – and fan out across northern New Jersey to speak at churches, synagogues and community centers about race issues. The operation was quite effective, attracting a great number of volunteers from colleges and the Jaycees civic organization. It was imperative that we work toward a more harmonious relationship between the black and white communities, considering all that Newark had just been through with the racial uprising.

It was a progressive movement and having the Jaycees on board gave the newly formed New Community Corporation the "Good Housekeeping" seal of approval. The Jaycees was a civic organization that promoted leadership skills among young people between the ages of 18-40, with an emphasis on community service. It was more formally known as the United States Junior Chamber, and carried a lot of clout. Monsignor Tom Carey and I spoke at rallies about race and this dialogue served as good public relations for attracting organizations like the Jaycees and funding opportunities for our New Community Corporation campaign to build new housing.

Operation Housewives: Babyland is Born

Out of Operation Understanding grew "Operation Housewives." Unlike what we see today on reality television, with the "Housewives of Orange County" or the "Housewives of Atlanta" and the "Housewives of New York," back in the day, real housewives solved real problems.

In the early 1960s, there was not one established licensed nursery program in the state. Although Mary Teresa Norton, the first woman Democrat from New Jersey to be elected to Congress in 1925, had started Queen's Daughter Day Nursery in 1912 in Jersey City. But the fact remains, that there was nothing affordable for black mothers in need of infant care. This caused tremendous strife in the lives of black women living in the Central Ward when it came to employment, because there was no one to watch the kids. Like the men, who wanted to build affordable housing after the racial uprising, the women at Queen of Angels wanted to start a low-cost daycare program for Central Ward families.

In 1967, when you went to Scudder Homes, there was no telling what you would find – broken elevators, apartments without hot water, no heat. Can you imagine taking a shower again and again without hot water on a cold winter's morning? That was the normal living condition for many black people in public housing. I remember bringing food to one mother living in a cold-water flat apartment, who had just experienced the death of her child from pneumonia. She was still in the throes of grief and uncertainty, as she sat by the crib where her other baby was sleeping. There was a mesh covering over the crib to prevent the rats from harming this child.

Mary Smith, who was the sister-in-law of Joe Chaneyfield, knew this scenario all too well. She was a resident of Scudder Homes, along with her husband and four children. Mary and her family lived on the seventh floor of Scudder Homes and she helped change the tide of how people living in public housing were treated. Mary was fed-up and determined to fight back, enough so that she formed a tenant association at Scudder Homes.

Mary's efforts with regard to Operation Housewives were the catalyst that caught the attention of white suburban women. Mary and other women started speaking out at suburban churches. It was there that white women heard for themselves the plight of black women living in public housing. Woman to woman, they were engaged, and these white women wanted to get involved to help. In an effort to heal the antagonistic relationship that existed between the races, the women got together for a series of discussions to acquaint themselves with one another and formed a "coffee klatch."

My dear friend Madge Wilson, a board member and outreach coordinator for New Community whom I've known for fifty years, was part of the group. In the following passage she lends her voice to the story of Operation Housewives, which was a reflection of God's love and a manifesto of truth and harmony:

> Mary Smith fought for us. She went to Trenton and let the powers that be know that we needed decent homes for our people. If there was a family with five or six kids, she wanted them to have housing with four bedrooms, a den and a utility room. The same as the average working white family had.
>
> I lived in the Stella Wright housing projects on the sixth floor and I had two children. All of us, the black women who lived in the projects, our places were small so our coffee klatch met at the homes of the white women. One of the women was a registered nurse. She and her husband lived in South Orange and he didn't like the idea of black women being in

his home. We could tell just by the way he looked at us. His wife would tell us, "Oh disregard him." She didn't seem to mind if he heard her either.

We first were getting together and celebrating everybody's birthday and then we started doing small projects, like putting food baskets together for the poor. These were women of means so they could afford to pay for children from the Central Ward to go to summer camp and things like this. Their husbands were resourceful for helping people in the community get jobs. This was how many jobs came about in the community, through one of these women's husbands. It was almost like having our own employment service.

We kept having these discussions and they decided to work on something more significant than the small projects. They wanted to do something that would really benefit the community and help us to raise money toward a daycare program. This was always the basis for why we were coming together and, of course, we were doing other things also.

Under the name of Central West Service League, women like Ute Tellini and Gloria Biggs, as well as other white women, opened a thrift store at 302 South Orange Ave. Mary Smith, who started Operation Housewives, along with her mother, Inez Jenkins, worked in the store and provided a down home environment with home-cooked meals when we all gathered there. The white women stocked the store with high-priced clothes from stores like B. Altman, Bonwit Teller, Bergdorf Goodman and fancy boutiques in Millburn and Short Hills. There were all kinds of accessories and handbags, shoes you name it, good quality merchandise, with labels like Chanel and Dior. The proceeds from the store went toward paying the rent at the store.

With a $1,000 loan from the suburban housewives and a $500 loan from a suburban Presbyterian church, "Babyland" was founded in August 1969 in two basement apartments in the Scudder Homes projects. With the growth of Babyland,

Mary Smith became its director. The Newark Housing Authority donated the space and allowed us to knock down the wall that separated the two apartments to make a large open space, along with other rooms. The white women supplied the nursery with everything it needed.

Dr. Paul Kearny, whose wife was involved in Operation Housewives, was a pediatrician in Short Hills, and he volunteered on his day off every Wednesday at the nursery tending to the needs of these little black babies.

The joint venture between the women of Operation Housewives was a success. Babyland, under the umbrella of NCC, was the first of its kind to be recognized by the state as a certified licensed entity entrusted to the care of infants from 2 ½ months old to 2 ½ years old. Babyland set the standards for infant care in New Jersey and a precedent by pressing the state to examine its daycare policies to include infant care and to commit to the sharing of funding in that direction, which had never been done before. Women in the community now had an affordable and safe place to leave their children. This empowered them to seek permanent work and to attend school to better their lives.

I am grateful to Mary for her vision and to Madge for preserving that story, because Babyland grew to be a vital operation in fulfilling the needs of so many mothers and families in Newark. Babyland was a groundbreaking operation thanks to the legal help we received from attorneys Adrian Foley Jr. and John J. Gibbons. They used their legal savvy to help us in whatever way we needed in order to gain legitimate legislation, incorporation and authorization to be recognized by the federal and state government. Babyland would come to serve over 300 children through the federally funded Title XX Social Security Act program.

Babyland established one of the first daycare centers in the nation in 1989 that catered to children born with HIV/AIDS. Infectious diseases, this was an area that Dr. Leon Smith, who had volunteered at Queen of

Angels, specialized in. His work, along with that of Dr. James Oleske, who had been a student of Dr. Smith's, was invaluable to such a vulnerable population, children. Babyland also implemented a protective child-abuse program.

Furthermore, once Babyland was up and operating with government recognition, other people in the community took interest in it for dubious reasons. Members from the Temple of Kawaida, an organization that had been established to promote black culture, seemed to think that they should have a say-so in the operation of Babyland. They threatened and demanded to be a part of the governing board of Babyland. Their heightened interest boiled down to money. But their harassment of the women running the day-to-day operation of Babyland became an intolerable nuisance.

When Joe got wind of their unannounced visits and threats, he made sure he was on the scene regularly at Babyland. One day, when two fellows from the Temple of Kawaida showed up there, Joe put them both in headlocks underneath each arm and told them, "If I catch you over here again I'll break your necks."

That was the last we saw of them.

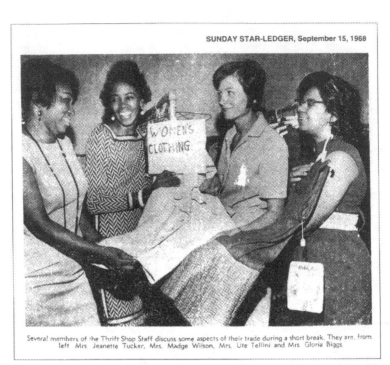

Several members of the Thrift Shop Staff discuss some aspects of their trade during a short break. They are, from left Mrs. Jeanette Tucker, Mrs. Madge Wilson, Mrs. Ute Tellini and Mrs. Gloria Biggs

Efforts of both urban and suburban thrift shop workers provided funding that enabled the first Babyland to open.

CHAPTER 10

Black Leadership: A Guiding Principle of New Community Corporation

But as for you, be strong and do not slack off, for there shall
be a reward for what you do – Chronicles 15:7

The newly created New Community Corporation drew its inspiration from President Lyndon Johnson's "War on Poverty." His administration's effort to build "The Great Society" was the impetus for us to dream of something great for the Central Ward. Our corporation's mission statement aligned with President Johnson's altruistic approach to aiding the poor: *To help residents of inner cities improve the quality of their lives to reflect individual, God-given dignity and personal achievement.*

The president melded the political and social needs of those living in dire poverty by creating the multifunctional Office of Economic Opportunity (OEO). Through this office, social programs such as food stamps, Medicare and Medicaid, as well as the Head Start education program for youngsters, were made available to the underserved. These programs were essential in helping many of the parishioners at Queen of Angels, many who were living in dire poverty in the Central Ward. These programs helped so many people breathe a sigh of relief, especially the elderly.

The Office of Economic Opportunity trickled down to Queen of Angels. Through the United Community Corporation, founded by Cyril Tyson, one of the first non-profit community action agencies in Newark, we received funding for a small piloted summer reading program at the church. The program was created for black high school students who were reading far below their grade level. There happened to be a number of basketball players from Central High School that participated in the program. Our summer program helped to prepare these students for college. For others who received offers to play basketball in Europe, it made them more literate. A unique part of the program involved six women who were on welfare that we hired as teacher aides to help the students. We then followed the women's journeys and some of them ended up doing very well, with the experience pointing them in the direction to start careers. When people are given an opportunity, they rise to the occasion.

The long tradition of the Roman Catholic Diocese providing opportunity and aid to those less fortunate made Queen of Angels and New Community a nice fit for the Mount Carmel Guild. The guild was the official social service agency of the Newark Roman Catholic Archdiocese. It had a national reputation for its work, particularly in the area of special needs for the blind and deaf. We thought we could link New Community's development agenda to the Mount Carmel Guild. We believed that our service to the community was vital. The guild was large and had the resources and the ability to mobilize money. We needed to connect to their resources. We certainly couldn't build anything without money.

We soon discovered that the Mount Carmel Guild's idea of community development was worlds apart from ours. They had built one multiple dwelling of affordable housing, but they were not concerned with soliciting any input from the community. However, we still thought we could exist under the guild's umbrella. It was our hope that the diocesan would serve as the agency that would set up and sponsor our housing corporation.

The first thing we did was submit four names to the guild. The list was made up of people who were interested in being on the guild's policy-making board for housing development. They included members from the community and from Queen of Angels—all were black residents. Their names were promptly rejected and from there, our interactions with the guild turned hostile.

Willie displayed militant inclinations and thus served as our H.

Rap Brown, the radical activist who served as chairman of Student Non-Violent Coordinating Committee (SNCC) in 1967. Now the president of New Community and president of the United Afro American Association, Willie went on record with this statement in the Newark News on September 21, 1968: "I want the Catholic Church to show its concern for black people forced to live in substandard housing in the city of Newark. This area under consideration (the Central Ward) is one of the most rundown in the state." An undeniable rabble-rouser, Willie's voice served as our corporation's bullhorn. "I defy any agency or group to interfere with the project," he told the reporter. Willie would propose doing things like dumping rats in Military Park during the business day as a tactic to get people's attention. He was gravely serious about what we were intending to do—building a new community of common bonds—as was I.

Black leadership was one of the key elements of our proposal, which was sorely needed. It was important to our policy decision-making board for Black leadership to garner the respect of people from all walks of life. Therefore, Blacks had to be included in all aspects of the community development effort. And Willie, our undisputed leader, was one of those people. Participation from the black community was critical to our model for building a new community. However, the Mount Carmel Guild didn't see it that way. They staunchly opposed the inclusion of community members on their housing board.

Along with my priestly duties during this time, I was also attending Fordham University to work towards a master's degree in Sociology, while being nurtured and groomed by Father Fitzpatrick. I strived to achieve the type of inclusiveness in my work he emphasized in his book titled, *One Church Many Cultures: Challenges of Diversity*. As part of my studies, I had written a paper that explained two levels of leadership - citywide and hyper-local. I learned that, universally, a good leader must be respected by the entire community—including people from all walks of life.

Our attempt to bring the social and religious sectors together was hastily rejected by the Mount Carmel Guild. It became clear that the Mount Carmel Guild was not interested in promoting Black leadership.

The people from the community, for the last two years, had been a vital part of the discussion and planning for a new community. However, once the Mount Carmel Guild rejected the names of candidates put forth, it directly challenged New Community Corporation's objective to model inclusiveness. If we had gone along with the guild's program, it would have been the same as if the New Community board had said: *"Oh, your ideas are not important or good enough."* That would have served as a slap in the face to all those people who had put their trust in what we were doing - building a community together.

We asked community members, "If you had the opportunity to move out of substandard housing would you?" We got a resounding "Yes!" That was our starting point in forming a partnership with the potential tenants of the first proposed New Community property. Since I had arrived in Newark, the Newark Roman Catholic Archdiocese had not embraced its black parishioners and residents in ways that considered the needs of the community. Could that have been because it was an all-black parish? Queen of Angels was not only a magical place, it was part of the archdiocese, and a popular church, but it was not made to feel that way. That did not sit well with me.

In the end, we were left to fend for ourselves. As the newly formed New Community Corporation board of directors, we would have to come up with the funding for the proposed development project. What had once seemed hopeful - the archdiocese potentially funding our project - was now null and void.

CHAPTER 11

Discovering Africa and the Roots of Black Nationalism

Bearing with one another and forgiving one another;
as the Lord has forgiven you, so must you also do. And
over all these put on love, that is, the bond of perfection.
– Colossians 3:13-14

Black Nationalism was on the rise internationally, as well as on the national and local stage. With the rise of the Black Power Movement, people such as Newark's native son, Amiri Baraka, were able to affect change. Baraka helped found the Congress of African People (CAP) in 1970, modeling the organization after the Organization of African Unity. He was also one of the leaders of the Temple of Kawaida in Newark that represented the Swahili expression of values and traditions specific to African cultural mores. In fact, on the day that I was ordained as a priest May 25, 1963, 32 independent nations of Africa formed the Organization of African Unity. This international movement promoted black solidarity and was represented by an amalgamation of black people both globally and here in the United States.

Was it a coincidence that all this African unification was occurring at the same time I became immersed in the black community in Newark? No, this was God's work and I was ready for his calling. I walked the streets of the Central Ward every day after the Summer Disorders. With the rise of the Black Power Movement, the community's cultural identity became resurrected and collective consciousness rejuvenated.

Collectively, the black race was breaking free from a passive second-class citizenry to be recognized as first-class human beings. The chant "Black is beautiful" resonated among young people. The image of a raised fist became the iconic symbol of black power and the Black Panthers. "This is Madness," by The Last Poets, the original spoken word artists, provided a wake-up call for the masses. In traditional African dress, the brightly colored dashikis and African-inspired fabrics adorned by women and men sporting kufis symbolized a connection to the motherland of Africa, similarly to how yarmulkes linked Jewish men to Israel. And the sights and sounds of the city captured the same vitality as seen in a Jacob Lawrence painting – a spirited people in motion, doing and being against all odds.

Black Nationalism in Newark was especially on display with the strong presence of the Nation of Islam's black Muslims. They played an important role in spiritually rehabilitating black males, particularly those who had been incarcerated. The group also promoted strong family values, despite the philandering shenanigans of their leader, Elijah Muhammad. The Nation of Islam was highly visible and the newspaper "Muhammad Speaks," and garnered a strong allegiance of followers with a forceful rhetoric for economic development. The group established businesses and Newark's Mosque No. 25 opened a school. In my opinion, the black Muslims formed a united front that appeared much stronger than what I saw in the splintered Baptist church.

During the late '60s and into the '70s, community development became big business, as a result of President Johnson's "War on Poverty," and the black power movement hitched itself to the political synergy. Through the Office of Equal Opportunity (OEO), funds allocated for "urban renewal" land development projects sparked a competitive surge from churches and community action groups jockeying to get into the affordable housing game. The OEO also helped to fund day care, cultural arts programs and numerous other services.

By this time, Amiri Baraka had returned home to Newark from his artistic sojourn in New York's Greenwich Village. Amid the rise of community development, Baraka's acclaim as a poet and a celebrated playwright - with an Obie Award for his 1964 play "Dutchman" - boosted his name and status in the city. His message, as an artist and activist, emphasized black aesthetics and attracted a cross-section of people from black militants to white intellectuals. Just as his play "Dutchman" raised the issue of race in the most provocative way – through depicting a heated subway conversation between a black man and white woman – the issue of race relations was becoming the central focus of a brewing political firestorm.

Baraka and members of the Temple of Kawaida were met with resistance when they tried to build Kawaida Towers. The proposed community development project was slated to be built in Newark's North Ward, which was predominantly an Italian community. That was until Stephen Audubato Sr., who was making a name for himself in the North Ward, opposed the idea of black nationalists erecting a building with an African connotation in an Italian neighborhood.

"What would happen if the Italians got funds to build an apartment building in the Central Ward and called it the Garibaldi Building," said Audubato, according to Julia Rabig, author of "Fighting Deadly Cycles and Crippling Powerlessness: The Democratization of Expertise in the Community Development Movement of Newark, N.J." State Assemblyman Anthony Imperiale, a one-time proponent for the project, changed course when he was confronted by Audubato, the aggressive new kid on the block. Imperiale shifted his political weight in opposition to the project and the Kawaida Towers construction site was shutdown.

In developing the idea for New Community, we were promoting an inclusive approach to community building, however it was evident that race was still an ugly issue in Newark. Baraka and his followers defined themselves as separatists. Their ideology clashed with ideas held by myself and other board members of New Community, particularly Joe, because we were trying to bring a coalition of all races together. However, what struck me about Baraka was his frequent referencing of Mwalimu Julius Nyerere, the president of Tanzania. The Pan-African model of community building that Nyerere defined as "African communalism" was Baraka's mantra for "self-determination."

What was this "African communalism" all about, I wondered? Self-determination was an important element attached to the zeitgeist of

Black Nationalism in America and was also an important tenet of New Community. Self-determination, in my view, was not an anti-white thing, but rather an ideology that enhanced growth while affirming the relevancy of black participation on all levels in society. I felt strongly that Baraka's separatist rhetoric amplified the racial divide. His angst with the white establishment was not directed at me and yet on some level I still took it personally, considering my placement as a white priest at an all-black parish working to uplift the community I served. Truthfully speaking, Baraka was a thorn in my side.

Motivated by the expression to "keep your friends close and your enemies closer," I embarked on a trip to Africa to learn about self-determination and African communalism. Aside from my personal feelings towards Baraka, I was fueled to travel by an unquenchable thirst to understand all community development modalities. My trip to Africa ended up being an experience I would never forget.

Journey to Africa

In 1973, my month long journey took me to Ethiopia, Kenya and Tanzania, where I hoped to interview President Julius Nyerere about "African communalism." I employed all my personal and network connections to arrange a meeting. Peter Mutharika, who I had befriended when he was attending Yale University in Connecticut, was perhaps the most important of these contacts. His assistance in coordinating my travel plans was invaluable.

Peter's brother, Bingu wa Mutharika, was in charge of the United Nations East Africa with headquarters located in Ethiopia. Bingu wa Mutharika eventually would become the president of Malawi.

Just before departing for Africa, I received an urgent telegram from Peter where he instructed me to contact the United Nations East Africa. I was then informed that the USS Enterprise aircraft carrier was stationed in the Indian Ocean, along the coast of East Africa, and the situation in the region was getting heated. Peter had made arrangements for me to check into a hotel once I arrived in Ethiopia. It was not safe for me to stay in the airport while anticipating flying on to Dares

Salam, Tanzania. Instead, when my plane landed at the Haile Selassie I International Airport in the middle of the night, I was immediately whisked off to the hotel. Thus, Ethiopia became the first leg of my trip.

As it turned out, my hotel room was located on the same floor as the Russian soccer team. Whenever I left my room, I recognized the same two men lurking in my vicinity. *Was this my imagination or am I being followed?* I thought. I eventually learned that the men were part of the KGB - Russia's equivalent of our FBI – and were surveiling my every move. What a comedic error, because I was the furthest thing from being a spy. Yes, I was on the prowl to gain valuable information, but nothing of interest to the KGB.

Emperor Haile Selassie (ruled 1930-1974) was still governing Ethiopia when I was there. Although I didn't get to meet him, I had the privilege of meeting a number of his government officials. What blew my mind was the discovery that Emperor Selassie was the founder of the Organization for African Unity. He was the first chairperson of the organization that was born on the very same day I was ordained as a priest. In my mind, I pictured my emerging relationship with the African Diaspora developing in tandem with the solidarity displayed between Africa (with African communalism) and America (with the Black Power Movement). The OAU was formed to improve the living conditions of African people, ensure their sovereignty and rid Africa of colonialism. These were the same ideals Black Americans were fighting for. My endearing love for the black residents in the Central Ward and beyond was magnified by the spirituality and the humanity of all the people I came in contact with while in Africa.

I also had the opportunity to spend a day with the chancellor of the Coptic Church in Ethiopia. The history of the religion was fascinating. The roots of Christianity in Ethiopia, I learned, particularly Coptic Christianity, dated much further back than Islam. Coptic Christianity was an offshoot of the Ethiopian Orthodox Church, which believed that the "Person of Christ," was divine but also a fallible human being. The Coptics believed Christ's divine nature and human nature were one in the same.

Coptic Christianity, during my time spent in Ethiopia, appeared to be celebrating a revival. What I found fascinating was the discovery that the Coptic footprint was deeply entrenched in the Caribbean island of Jamaica. Emperor Haile Selassie, a practicing Coptic, was revered as the "Divine" by his Jamaican followers, known as *Rastafarians*. I learned that *"Ras,"* the Amharic translation for "leader," was attached to *Tafari* (Makonnen), the emperor's given name at birth. The *Rastafarians* in Ethiopia and Jamaica praised Emperor Selassie's holy name. The fundamental basis of Coptic Christianity was not much different from Catholicism, with service work and liturgy as the primary route to salvation.

Further along in my visit, I ventured out to a village in Ethiopia where the people had established a growing economy. The villagers were able to produce cloth with weaving equipment that had been donated by Scandinavians. This valuable commodity allowed them to become self-sufficient. They took great pride in what they were doing and the end result was the building of a school. To me, that was quite impressive. I always felt education was essential to economic development and in this village the spirit of self-sufficiency and education was fully on display. I filed in my memory bank all that was possible for when I returned home to Newark.

The next leg of my trip took me to Kenya, which proved to be a defining part of my journey. Before I left America, Peter had put me in touch with a black woman from Harlem whose friend, an Australian man, was a commissioner (equivalent of a diplomat) to Kenya. I connected with him immediately upon arriving in Kenya. His headquarters were located in Nairobi, and he took me by his office, where they happened to be installing a new archbishop for their newly formed archdiocese. I was surprised that the program was being performed in English instead of Swahili.

Kenya's beautiful topography boasted pristine greenery that was flush with the fertile crops of tea and coffee that supported the Kenyan economy. In the outlying villages, tribal chiefs ruled like political bosses. I met one of the village chiefs, and despite my not understanding the KiKuyu language, we had a conversation comprised of charade-like gestures and eye contact. And yet we managed to get our point across to each other. This, for me, affirmed the power of the human connection.

Kenya had gained its independence from British rule on December 12, 1963, when Prime Minister Jomo Kenyatta (ruled 1964-1978) was elected as the country's first president on June 1, 1964. Kenyatta, who was in office during my trip, promoted the ideology of "reconciliation" between the races and native tribes. He promoted reconciliation in terms of Kenyan political organizations putting aside their differences, a position, he summed up nicely with a national slogan that he coined, *"Harambbee,"* which means to "pull together." That certainly seemed to be the pathway to understanding we were all in this together. Kenyatta led by example, by including all races (black, white and Asian) in the government. And although independent from colonial rule, Kenya still maintained a heartening connection to Britain. What impressed me about the country was the togetherness I witnessed among the black and white races.

Unfortunately, there was very little pulling together in the United States or Newark. The races were divided like partisan political organizations. The Temple of Kwaida openly promoted the separation of the races. The scene in Kenya was much different from what I was used to seeing.

The last leg of the trip brought me to Tanzania, where I had hoped to meet with President Julius Nyerere (ruled 1961-1985) to get my own take on his policy of "African communalism." Though I never landed an actual interview with the president, I met with a cabinet member of President Nyerere's administration. The administration explained the policy and how it centered on self-reliance, much in the same vein as New Community's ideology of self-sufficiency. African communalism included the villagers – villages where the state had jurisdiction - as part of the decision-making process. The country was a province of democracy and the communal will of its people. This, too, modeled what we were attempting at New Community with our "villagers," the residents of the Central Ward.

The ideas that we were discussing around the table at New Community for years had been actualized in Africa. By including the people in the decision-making process, a sense of pride became evident. I met many people while visiting Tanzania and not once did I sense, feel, see or hear even a modicum of divisiveness between the black and white races, despite the country's history of colonization.

My pilgrimage to Africa strengthened my need to serve others and deepened my faith. I couldn't wait to get back to Newark to tell Joe all about my trip. There were times when Joe and I would talk about life, religion and, of course, Newark, for hours. When I finally arrived back in Newark, I told Joe that the radical Black Nationalist mandate here in America that promoted dividing the races was not what I had witnessed in Africa. New Community's ideology, I told him, should point towards "African communalism" and bringing people together rather than what Baraka and his followers were preaching.

Joe was proud of his African heritage and often joked about being called a "Geechee," having grown up in Ridgefield, South Carolina, before settling in Newark. This expression was ascribed to those South Carolinians who lived along the state's coast. But more importantly, Geechees upheld the language that was a throwback to the motherland.

"You know, Padre," Joe said, using the name he had always called me, "These supposedly militant folks talking that junk. This Amiri Baraka ... he yells, talking that white black thing. He hasn't built anything, but he can talk about what supposed to be happening in the city?"

Joe's response was right on. He welcomed me home and I was glad to see my dear friend. Joe was ready to roll up his sleeves and get to work and so was I. We were well aware of the uphill climb. After my trip to Africa, I was even more convinced that with community empowerment, as the mortar to bring the neighborhood together, New Community would build up the Central Ward, brick by brick and block by block.

CHAPTER 12

Community Empowerment

And training us to reject godless ways and worldly desires and to live temperately, justly, and devoutly in this age, as we await the blessed hope, the appearance of the glory of the great God and of our savior Jesus Christ – Titus 2:12-13

From my point of view, there was not enough emphasis being placed on the social needs of the people. For example, a family of six certainly needed more space than two bedrooms but in public housing that was the norm. Consequently, in conversation, I engaged board member, Arthur Bray, about how both the social and political needs should work together to benefit the residents in the community. As a result of my many discussions with Arthur, I was hired to work part-time with the Essex County Planning Board and worked there for five years. My job was to make sure the human dimension was accounted for in surveys taken by various groups, government agencies and so forth. This allowed a more realistic approach when it came to planning for housing, transportation and the other essential needs of communities.

My role with the Essex County Planning Board felt like a chance to act as a double-agent. I was able to infiltrate areas of government – the planning board being one example – to access inside information that was valuable to the work being done at New Community. I was able to bring information back to my constituency, the black community, and the information allowed us to keep pressing forward. People like Joe and Willie, as smart as they were, would not have gained access to the same places during that time simply because of their race

By the late '60s, we had laid out our ideas and conducted a poll of the first tenants for the proposed New Community housing development. They agreed to give up one Saturday a month for two years to discuss the in-depth professional planning necessary for developing new housing. That was the buy-in. If they consistently gave up one Saturday over the allotted period of time they were guaranteed a new apartment and input in the construction process. Arthur was our link to the Essex County planning office and his help was essential in putting together a total package that met the people's approval. Excitement began to build.

However, what the tenants were requesting was not a workable option. The pre-selected tenants wanted a single-story home with a white picket fence. Besides the single-home dwelling issue, there were other hurdles we had to jump. The people did not understand what the professional architect or government officials were laying out in regard to what they could or could not do. We needed to give the community a better understanding of the jargon and specifics of what was being created. It was apparent that we needed to set up a training program that would educate the prospective dwellers about balanced land use in accordance to what they wanted.

It was during this time that New Community procured its very first funding as land developers with a $13,000 grant from the New Jersey State Department of Community Affairs. The money was allocated to provide a training program to our first cohort of residents. We brought in the architect, Roger Glasgow, to speak to the group.

"No you can't do that," said Glasgow to those who were still set on having the house with the picket fence.

"We don't want a high-rise building" the residents grumbled back. Glasgow had been conditioned to follow the state's guidelines for public housing. He was talking about building towers up to 15 stories high.

Meanwhile, Oscar Newman, author of the book, *Defensible Space,* spent two Saturdays with the community. We served food and even had activities for the children. Oscar did a presentation on how to design housing with safety in mind - the do and don'ts. It was an interactive presentation with slides and more and lasted from 9 a.m. to 5 p.m.

The time had arrived for us to schematically work out our plans.

We agreed to build six buildings that would not exceed five stories and accommodated a center courtyard. Each building would have single loaded corridors, meaning there were no hallways, but rather elevated sidewalks with an outside wall that separated each unit's balcony.

Another safety measure was the placement of the mailboxes. They would be located in the center of the complex in a highly visible spot. One nearly unanimous request by the selected tenants was to have their own front door. These doors would be unlike those entombed in the typical public housing dwelling. For these tenants, being able to open their front door and see the light of day, or look out onto a courtyard, was a marquee feature. Also, the omission of interior hallways improved safety. The tenants wouldn't have to worry about strangers lurking in hallways outside their doors. By incorporating these concepts into the plan, the future tenants began to understand that density, with regard to multiple dwellings, could have a positive outcome on their quality of life and still look attractive.

The deputy director of planning working with us was a professional commercial artist, so he produced renderings of what the homes would look like. Called New Community Homes Court, the complex consisted of 120 units. As the community's input flowed, it fed into concepts that continued to move the project forward. Eventually, the ideas were put into a detailed 45-acre scale model of New Community. The vision was coming to life.

While the tenants were meeting, I spent a week engaged in classes that laid out the development of new cities. I also traveled to Holland and Germany to observe their planned cities. Garden towns seemed to be the new innovation. The irony in all of this was that there was a movement of garden towns actually starting locally in Fairlawn, New Jersey.

Upon first meeting Paul Yilvaker in 1967, when he served as the first Commissioner of Community Affairs for New Jersey, under Governor Hughes, he encouraged me to go back to graduate school. And when the state offered to pay my tuition to attend Fordham University, I couldn't refuse. It all seemed to fit together perfectly. I'm convinced that my steps were ordered to meet people such as Arthur Bray and Paul

Ylvisaker. They were like-minded in their passion and concern about the plight of inner cities.

Paul's friendship was valuable to what we were trying to do in Newark's Central Ward, where we implemented ideas he used in the development of the "New Model Cities" national program. Paul's words were quoted in a 1965 Life magazine article, and I can't help but marvel at their truth: "Men may find God in nature, but when they look at cities they are viewing themselves. And what Americans see mirrored in their cities these days is not very flattering."

CHAPTER 13

Uncharted Territory: NCC Land Developers

My God will fully supply whatever you need, in accord with his glorious riches in Christ Jesus -Philippians 4:19

The New Community Foundation was formed in 1969 as part of a concerted effort to strictly raise money for the corporation. The foundation managed to attract a broad base of suburban support as a result of the Operation Understanding and Operation Housewives campaigns, involving the Jaycees Civic Organization. The foundation had a dual purpose: To raise funds and create a wide base of political support. Herman G. Haenlisch, who was a Methodist, became its president.

"This is a white-help-black project," Herman informed the local newspaper about the foundation. "But it is not a white-tell-the-blacks-what-to-do project. The people living in the Central Ward don't have any bootstraps to pull themselves up with. We hope to get those bootstraps through this fund drive."

The foundation spearheaded a project that was the genesis of a Hebrew Rabbinical student who was assigned to work in an urban environment. He interned with New Community during the summer. The foundation sold certificates that were really donations for a square foot of land. His suggestion was modeled after the "Israel Tree" campaign, which was successful in getting countless numbers of Jewish people, as well as others, to be attached to the rebuilding of Israel.

In our case, everyone who donated five dollars received one certificate or one "honorary" share for their money. In all, about $100,000 was raised through this effort. In a unique way, the initiative allowed suburban people to be a part of the change in Newark. It also gave them a strong vested interest in seeing the effort to build housing for those in dire need become a reality. Each suburban community developed its own program for raising money.

By June of 1971, 15 local chapters of the Jaycees made up of 3,500 people, had organized fund-raising drives for the New Community Foundation. People like Bob Lilley, the head of Governor Hughes' commission on the '67 Summer Disorders, sent letters out soliciting funds for New Community. In Berkeley Heights, the Jaycees spearheaded a door-to-door campaign. While in Park Ridge, New Jersey, the churches got together, along with the Girl and Boy Scouts, to raise funds. We had great ecumenical activity appealing to churches, synagogues and other civic organizations.

The Jaycees, in particular, played an invaluable role in linking the New Community Foundation to countless contacts, especially after they adopted our campaign as a statewide project. They became our social networking model long before Facebook and Twitter existed.

One of those contacts was Engelhard Industries, located in Iselin, New Jersey. It offered to make a substantial grant to New Community to support a youth project. The board for the New Community Foundation decided that they would refuse the grant. Instead, they chose to ask Engelhard Industries for a $200,000 loan in November of 1971. The same request had been promptly denied years before by the Newark Roman Catholic Archdiocese, when Willie and other New Community board members approached Archbishop Thomas Boland.

Engelhard Industries approved our loan request. It was agreed upon that the loan would have no time constriction and no interest payment, because at that point the foundation wasn't sure how long it would take to get the project actuated. Accruing interest on the loan would run counter to what we were trying to accomplish. The basis of the loan was to create credit on the part of New Community; this credit would help to make the group more responsible towards its own resources and would also predispose New Community Corporation to borrow money and to repay it.

We asked Mr. Charles Engelhard if we could have access to his company's department heads, especially the heads of the real estate, legal and engineering departments. Though initially surprised, Engelhard seemed pleased by our unusual request and, again, he agreed. In fact, he assigned his own counsel to work as a liaison between New Community and Engelhard Industries so that they could be of greater assistance in developing our housing project. With these professionals on board, we gained experienced leadership that infused confidence in our efforts. None of us knew anything about developing housing but over the course of two years, we had learned an awful lot. But there was much more to learn.

We decided to hire one of the top people in the field of housing as a consultant on a monthly retainer basis. Then we sought out an architectural firm. We hired a minority firm based in New York to develop the plans for the first units of housing. One of the big eight accounting firms, Ernst and Young, was asked to be the auditors for New Community. Our board considered a yearly audited statement of the finances as an absolutely necessary task. The integrity of the operation was a priority and that still holds true today.

The largest law firm in the state, McCarter and English, took over the legal reins from Engelhard and assigned Steven B. Hoskins as our lawyer for the housing project. New Community deftly managed to hitch itself to high-level technical assistance. This allowed us to be taken more seriously in the land development arena. We were in *this* game for keeps. With the quality of help we had assembled, our naysayers could no longer dismiss us so easily. Further, with an eye for engineering from my days spent at Manhattan College, I enjoyed a front row seat to witness the integral workings of land development.

When New Community was struggling to formalize its plan, the Victoria Foundation provided us with a start-up grant that allowed us to open our first office space at 755 South Orange Avenue, which was located upstairs from Babyland. As the Victoria Foundation explored the needs of the Central Ward and how it could best help, the foundation recognized the potential impact that New Community could have in helping those living there.

With the grant from the Victoria Foundation, we were also able to hire our first employee, Cecilia Faulks, in 1973. In the beginning, Cecilia answered the telephone and took messages. As we progressed in the area of land development, she became vital to the day-to-day operation of the corporation. She also proved to be vital in high stakes situations. Tempers had a way of flaring at some of our spirited board meetings.

At one particular board meeting, Willie, who was the president of New Community and had a way of pushing people's buttons, had missed a good portion of a meeting. When he finally arrived, he wanted a recap and Joe told Willie that he should have been there at the start. Willie made a smart remark and tempers flared. Joe tore into Willie like a bulldozer into a brick building and none of us could break them up. At that moment, Cecilia knelt down on the floor where Joe was choking the life out of Willie and managed to get in between the two men. Because Joe would not physically harm a woman, Cecilia was able to bring him back from the brink of destruction and Willie's demise. I was grateful for Cecilia because it might have been a totally different outcome had she not been on the scene. Personifying grace in motion, Cecilia rose in the ranks to eventually become the director of human resources at New Community. Not only did she excel at her own duties, Cecilia kept everyone in check.

In our ongoing quest as land developers, New Community made the choice to go the private land-purchase route in order to avoid getting bogged down in politics and bureaucracy of the urban renewal process. Most of the developments in Newark, particularly those related to either the United States Housing and Urban Development (HUD) subsidies or connected to state financing, were built on urban renewal land. At one point, Newark was the king of urban renewal land development in the country, however it also was one of the most political. Large for-profit developers were given carte blanche commitments by the city for huge parcels of land. This was one of the outcries from the '67 Summer Disorders, the fact that one developer controlled over 100 acres in Newark's Central Ward and had no plans to use the land. These commitments were often given by the city for political or financial reasons. New Community was determined to stay far away from that morally corrupt arena.

New Community's decision to forgo the urban renewal route caused the land price for our project to jump significantly. The New Community board had identified 45 acres just south of the University of Medicine and Dentistry of New Jersey, where 97 percent of the buildings on the land were structurally substandard. Thus the board aimed to stake claim there. However, before the land could be purchased, we found ourselves entangled in a web of land ownership disputes regarding who owned the parcels of land on the 45 acre tract.

The Ronson Corporation, a manufacturer of handsome-looking cigarette lighters, was one of the owners with whom we faced the most difficult negotiations. The building was abandoned, thus of negative value, and the property was also an environmental mess to clean up. Governor Hughes and Bob Lilley, President of New Jersey Bell, tried to intervene and help settle the situation. Their efforts did not work. Finally, Willie, NCC's own version of Civil Rights activist H. Rap Brown, threatened to occupy the company's offices in Woodbridge, New Jersey. Governor Hughes let it be known that whatever happened, the company was on its own and should not expect any protection from the state. Shortly thereafter, Ronson released their hold on the land.

The fundraising effort of the New Community Foundation paid off and we gained access to $90,000 in a private write-down cost of the land. With the financial assistance of Englehard Industries, we were able to purchase the first two acres of land to start the building process. To cut down on costs for the project, we handled our own demolition of the site.

To the naked eye, the Central Ward was a gigantic, blighted eyesore with no potential. The city was the brunt of all sorts of jokes. On a return flight from a conference, I remember the flight attendant poking fun at Newark as we made our descent into Newark Liberty International Airport. "Welcome to the vacation capital of the world, Newark, New Jersey," he said sarcastically. Prior to the summer uprising, and certainly in the aftermath, people abandoned Newark in droves. New Community, in contrast, staked a claim in the city. My vision for Newark went far beyond what the eye could see. With funds raised by the New Community Foundation, we purchased large parcels of land in the Central Ward, mostly at very low costs at public auctions. We were now in position to rebuild Newark's Central Ward.

We hired a consulting firm in New York City that handled land requisitions that we needed to be processed for land development. However, it had been my vision to groom New Community's workers to fit the needs of the corporation. The goal was self-sufficiency and it started first with Cecilia. She trained for a couple of weeks in New York with the consulting firm we had hired and learned how to process the land requisitions. That made it official: New Community was in the land development business.

PART II

CHAPTER 14

New Community Homes Court: A Dream Realized

Do nothing out of selfishness or out of vainglory; rather, humbly regard others as more important than yourselves, each looking out not for his own interests, but also everyone for those of others - Philippians 2:3-4

The structural height of our plans for New Community Homes Court called for a five-story building, while the state policy for public housing typically mandated high-rise towers. According to the state, which patterned its housing model after U.S. Department of Housing and Urban Development, it was more cost effective and efficient to erect high-rise buildings as opposed to the low-rise structure that New Community had planned.

We could talk all we wanted to, but this was put-up or shut-up. We now had to get the funding to build the structures. We had secured the land and now needed to make New Community Homes Court a reality, which required additional funding. The New Jersey Housing and Mortgage Finance Agency, which New Community had appealed to for funding, followed guidelines that ultimately promoted quantity over quality. The number of bedrooms per unit was not important to the mortgage financing agency. Our design for Homes Court was very attractive and had a garden apartment appearance that was not traditional, neither to the practices of the state nor landscape of the Central Ward.

The state director of housing, John Renna, didn't want to veer away from the guidelines for housing in New Jersey. And besides, the state legislature was under a Republican majority and to green light the project would have certainly attracted Democratic votes for the project. It was a political game being played with human beings. This created an exhausting web of bureaucracy. Indeed, if we were to ever secure funding for the project, New Community would be expected to meet certain criteria outlined by the state, and already we were at an impasse with the state. At one point, Renna had said to me: "Housing for poor people should look poor." His statement blew me away. It was during such times that I leaned most on my faith and, like my mother, kept persistent and patient in prayer.

> Blessed is the man who does not walk in counsel of the wicked, nor stand in the way of sinners, nor sit in the company with scoffers. Rather the law of the Lord is the joy and on his law he meditates day and night. (Psalm 1:1-2)

I had to rely on Scripture to deal with the distance between the ideal and the extreme. As far as the state was concerned, poor black people were not worthy of hope, only dreams deferred.

However, the network that New Community had built over the years served us well. The people from the suburbs wrote letters and called the state-run mortgage agency to inquire about when the project would be approved. We had strong advocacy and strength in numbers, which helped us move toward a positive outcome. Renna told me he had never been so pressured. The CEOs of civic-minded companies were calling citizens in their suburban communities to root us on.

The back and forth between New Community and the state went on for so long that eventually, a new governor took office. The administration of Governor Brendan Byrne (1974-1982), a Democrat, was now in control of the New Jersey Housing and Mortgage Finance Agency. Bill Johnson had taken over the helm and one day I received a telephone call from him "I'm going to be up in Newark," Johnson said. "Let's get together. I want to talk to you." I didn't know him well, but Johnson continued: "You know we have the same enemy." Now I was all ears. Come to find out, Johnson previously worked for the New Jersey Housing and Mortgage Finance Agency, had quit and now he was back. Johnson declared that he was willing to step up and become an ally of New Community.

"I want to work with you," he said. "And by the way I agree with you. We need to put more into the quality of this housing. There's no point in using the HUD model. It doesn't work and there's no use in us following it." When the moment is ripe, righteous things have a way of happening, I thought to myself.

Under Johnson, the agency sought to create amenities that would change how people viewed low to moderate income housing. This was right up my alley. The agency's budget allotted for more landscaping than it had ever allowed before. The beautification of the grounds would be aesthetically pleasing to the tenants. The presentation of trees and beautiful shrubbery would be a deviation from the concrete norm. There was a gentle tranquility to the space that made it quite appealing, right in the heart of Newark.

After two years of planning and three years of fighting through the minutia of bureaucracy, New Community emerged successful and crossed the finish line. The money that was borrowed from Engelhard Industries was paid at the closing of the mortgage in September of 1972, for the first 120 units of New Community Homes Court.

In October of 1973, New Community broke ground on a two-acre site for Homes Court. The total cost of the project was $4.5 million. Homes Court consisted of six brick-faced buildings that were fireproof, with safety being an important concept, and the center courtyard serving as an asset for both community-building and aesthetics. It was an area where children could play just a blink away from their parents' watchful eye. The project was finished and occupied in October of 1975.

With the Christmas holiday nearing, a formal dedication took place for Homes Court on December 13, 1975. After laboring for 10 years--from the first idea to build a new community to this moment of completion--I was overjoyed with the sense that love, the highest caliber of human expression, had triumphed. Living up to Dr. King's dream, New Community proved that it was possible for people from every segment of society, every race and creed, to come together for the greater good of all God's people. It was a huge moment for the New Community board of directors, as well as the corporation's foundation, because we realized that our mission was about so much more than just building housing. I couldn't think of a better way to celebrate Christ's birth.

MONSIGNOR WILLIAM J. LINDER

CHAPTER 15

Jazz for the Masses

Let the word of Christ dwell in you richly, as in all wisdom you teach and admonish one another, singing psalms, hymns and spiritual songs with gratitude in your hearts to God – Colossians 3:16

I have a great appreciation for jazz and for the African-American contribution to this rich history. Barbara Kukla, who worked for many years at the *Star-Ledger* newspaper, has written extensively about Newark's jazz scene. Newark was home to many jazz greats like Sarah Vaughn, Wayne Shorter and James Moody, along with others. Kukla's most recent book, *America's Music: Jazz in Newark,* gives the city its much deserved prominence in the world of jazz history. While Amiri Baraka's book, *Digging: The Afro-American Soul of American Classical Music,* elevates the significance of jazz in American culture. From Louis Jordan's "Jump Jazz" to Louis "Satchmo" Armstrong, the legendary Charlie Parker, Lester Young – known as the "Pres" – short for president, because of his masterful work on the tenor sax. Art Blakey and the Modern Jazz Quartet to Sonny Rollins, Miles and contemporaries like Wynton Marsalis - the list is almost infinite. The indelible mark on the legacy of this music also includes Mary Lou Williams.

The Cookery in Greenwich Village was a place I frequented back in the early 70's. It was one of my favorite hangouts, where I'd catch performances by the great jazz pianist and composer, Mary Lou Williams. She and I eventually met through a mutual friend and became friends.

When I would show up at the Cookery and she heard my voice, Mary Lou would play one of my favorite melodies.

Mary Lou was also Catholic and I decided to extend an invitation for her to perform a jazz mass as a novel way to engage the community. To have someone of Mary Lou's stature play at the church would be a great honor. Mary Lou accepted my invitation.

After ironing out all the contractual details, Mary Lou still had one more stipulation: She would only play on a Baldwin piano. Unfortunately, the church did not own one. Thankfully, during the early '70's while I was working part-time with the Essex County Planning Board, I brought in extra income in addition to my priest salary. I applied for and was granted a loan to purchase a Baldwin baby grand piano for the church. What the church received in return was well worth the thousands of dollars spent.

Queen of Angels' relationship with Mary Lou continued and in 1972 she played at the church for seven Sundays during the entire Lenten Season. Then there was the finale Easter Sunday jazz Mass. With Mary Lou on the keys and a full choir and jazz band accompaniment, the church was swinging. Mary Lou was close friends with the great trumpeter Dizzy Gillespie, and she had invited him to perform at the church as well. She performed her composition, "Mary Lou's Mass," a popular jazz mass number. When Easter Sunday Mass was over and all the parishioners had gone home, I was treated to a solo concert by the incomparable Gillespie. For those seven weeks, my friend Mary Lou Williams, who died in 1981, transformed the church into a jazz haven for the masses

By the mid-'80s, New Community was well into the swing of land development. Like the rhythm of jazz music, we came up with improvisational ideas for revitalizing the community and creating new job opportunities. As a big fan of jazz, I thought: *Wouldn't it be nice to have a classy spot right here in the community where residents can go out and have dinner and hear live jazz?* After all, Newark was not only home to great jazz musicians, but it's been home to the premiere jazz radio station, WBGO-88.3, since 1979.

My vision for a jazz venue set my sight on the old St. Joseph Parish, where I was exiled to in 1973, after being removed from Queen of Angels. By the mid-'80s, St. Joseph Parish was vacant. The church had lost its base of people after the '67 summer uprising. Its close proximity to Essex County College, Rutgers University and several county buildings, made it a good location for a fine new dining spot and jazz club.

The beautiful brownstone façade and ecclesiastical architecture of the old St. Joseph Church made it a novel showcase. I brought my idea to the New Community board of directors, and as I hoped, the proposal was music to their ears. We agreed that the space could be developed to include commercial offices and simultaneously used as the corporation's headquarters. I remember taking our human resource director, Cecilia Faulks, to see the space. I explained my vision for the church to her, pointing to where the glass encased elevator would go, the winding staircase, offices, the jazz club and so forth. "Okay, if you say so, Father Linder," she said hesitantly. It was as if she was thinking: *I wish I could see what he does.* St. Joseph Plaza, the name we decided upon for the space, was a fascinating concept for out-of-towners as well as community residents. The idea of a restaurant jazz club, plus the occasional art exhibit, harmonized with New Community's commitment to promote the arts, especially in ways that reached the greater community. It would also create more job opportunities for Newark residents.

As expected, there were financial obstacles to overcome. And as far as the financial institutions were concerned, my idea was too novel and they were hands-off. The fact that the board considered it a good investment in the community was all that truly mattered. There were some pretty strong characters on the board and being denied financial backing had never stopped us before, so why would we let it now? I've never been one to accept no for an answer. My motto has always been, "Don't take 'no' from someone who can't give you a 'yes.'" Since the commercial banks didn't want anything to do with us, we went another route to get financing.

That alternate route took us straight to the office of Governor Thomas Kean, a Republican. Governor Kean allowed New Community, which has never claimed allegiance to any one political party, whether Democratic or Republican, to have access to several financial escrows that existed in our housing development fund that were tied to government bonds. This provided the funding we needed for the St. Joseph Plaza project that came with a $1.1 million mortgage.

The transformation of the vacant church into a revamped St. Joseph Plaza got underway in August of 1983. I was grateful for my friendship with Dominic Sciaretta of Claremont Construction, an old-school conservative who I managed to win over in my effort to develop the Central Ward. His sons, Donald and Stephen Sciaretta, who took over the family business after the untimely death of their father in 1981, attribute the compassionate side of their father to our friendship. They donated company resources and helped us to transform St. Joseph Church into St. Joseph Plaza.

The 24,000 square feet complex was designed with an open atrium and housed a number of administrative offices. The winding wooden staircase and three-story glass elevator served as conversation pieces. But the star of the show was the Priory Restaurant and jazz club. It offered a full-service lunch and dinner menu, including cocktails and wine and a popular Sunday brunch.

The grand opening ceremony of St. Joseph Plaza on April 18, 1985 was a spirited occasion. There was standing room only. Business leaders, professionals, dignitaries, family and friends from the community, all attended. I distinctly remember Bishop Joseph Francis, who served as the first black archbishop of the Newark Catholic Archdiocese, referring to the early pioneers of New Community Corporation as people of "vision and faith" in his address to the crowd.

Then Mayor Gibson, an original board member of NCC addressed the audience: "When we started the original corporation there were many people who said it couldn't be done. And the plans were too ambitious and since we had no money . . . they saw no prospects for success." In the eyes of many, the first New Community board of directors seemed to be a group of misfits. We had no money! But each board member vowed to commit to the endeavor for the long haul. And the gravity of the human potential with everyone working in harmony went beyond measure. In what was a rare reflective moment, my spirit was filled with an anointing of God's love. It was as if the mayor was reading my mind. He knew all too well what New Community had been through and had accomplished over the years. The rededication of St. Joseph Church now as St. Joseph Plaza was another one of God's miracles. But outside the doors of the plaza, many challenges remained.

The advent of vulture capitalism and globalization changed the face of corporate America. The lack of good prevailing wages for low-skilled workers and the evaporation of manufacturing jobs, contributed to a dire situation that eventually became ruled by the proliferation of drugs, deadly carjackings and a growing homeless population. There was a time when the numbers provided a harmless economic boost to the black community. But what was happening now was an unraveling of the social fabric that had an adverse effect on the community. Public education was deteriorating, incarceration numbers were climbing, the spread of HIV/AIDS took on epidemic proportions and black-on-black crime surged.

The new '80s era, amplified by a raucous beat, deafened the sweet sound of jazz.

MONSIGNOR WILLIAM J. LINDER

CHAPTER 16

The Politics of a New Community

Whoever cares for the poor lends to the Lord, who will pay back the sum in full – Proverbs 19:17

Politics had been a part of my life from almost the time I was in the crib. It was the dinner table conversation I heard growing up. My father was an active, politically connected Republican although Hudson County, where we lived, was primarily Democratic. Nevertheless, he was also a big fan of Frank Hague, the Democratic mayor of Jersey City. My father also believed in the book, "One World," by Wendell Wilkie, which expressed very liberal and progressive ideas. William Frederick Linder was a moderate Republican, unlike what we see today in this *nouveau* extremist Republican Party.

My father worked on local and senatorial campaigns in Hudson and Bergen counties and often took me with him to various political meetings. During election time, I was paid five dollars to retrieve the results from polling places and phone them into campaign headquarters, which was a lot of money back then, especially for a 10-year-old boy.

Dad would also drive the family annually down to Washington, D.C., where we would meet various members of Congress and their aides. During one of our visits, he arranged for us to meet New Jersey Senator Albert W. Hawkes, a personal friend. Visiting the nation's capital, where legendary leaders such as Washington, Jefferson and Lincoln lived in the form of mammoth-sized monuments, was a pretty spectacular experience for me.

When I arrived in Newark, however, and discovered the reality of politics under the Addonizio administration, spectacular was not the word that came to mind. To be more precise, what I saw of daily government and political affairs was downright sacrilegious. I knew from my upbringing that political representatives were supposed to look out for their citizens' best interest. In Newark, every man fended for himself. Truthfully speaking, when it came to New Community, we never fully trusted the local government, because we didn't want to be beholden to a system that we all knew was crooked.

That was until the dawning of a new day, when Kenneth Gibson was elected as the 34th mayor of Newark and its first black mayor. Gibson, unlike his predecessor, understood the urgency of repositioning political goals in tandem with a progressive social agenda. After all, before serving as mayor, he'd been the chief engineer for the Newark Housing Authority. He knew the housing situation all too well, and as a former NCC board member, he knew what we were all about.

During Mayor Gibson's tenure (1970 - 1986), New Community invested heavily in Newark's revitalization. In 1977, construction began on New Community Associates, a 225-unit building for the elderly. That was followed by the acquisition of Roseville, which, too, was for seniors. These were the first two of six senior citizen residences that New Community acquired and built. Unlike the occupants of Homes Court, who were adamant about not living in high-rise buildings, the seniors preferred that type of arrangement. Roseville, a former "old-age" home, as they were once called, had been run by the Little Sisters of the Poor, and offered the seniors a safer environment. People could not just walk up to their front door. The senior citizen buildings were secure and offered all the amenities they needed, including handicap accessibility, laundry facilities, a community room and a full-time care coordinator, from New Community's Department of Health and Social Services, to monitor their health and well-being.

Under the Gibson administration, my access to local, state and federal agencies increased. Indeed, my father would have gotten a real kick out of what I was doing, because it was his heart's desire for me to work in public service, preferably in government. Neither of us could have known then that my desire to be a priest would lead me to be the treasurer for the Essex County Improvement Authority, chairman of the Housing Task Force and a board member of the New Jersey Housing and Mortgage Finance Agency. My involvement with these government agencies – as well as the Urban Development Resources of Newark, where I chaired its project committee – fed my insatiable desire to understand all aspects of land development.

New Community was a perfect fit for Gibson's agenda and simultaneously served to legitimize the mayor's efforts in the area of housing, while restoring hope and trust between Newark residents and the city. Mayor Gibson established the non-profit Housing Redevelopment Program and appointed 27-year-old Tom Massaro as its director. Massaro and the mayor developed a close relationship, somewhat akin to father and son. Mayor Gibson linked the Housing Redevelopment Program to the state, helping to create and expand low-income housing through the federally funded Section 8 program. Massaro then appointed me to the executive committee of the non-profit housing program.

As a priest, I was in a unique position. I had given up all worldly possessions to serve God and the people. That made me work even harder than if I had been tied to my secular self. After all, my material needs were met –clothing, housing, food – what else did I need? The fierce competition in the bubble of land development was a political war zone of bureaucratic minefields and my platform of righteousness proved to be my best offense and defense. Being a priest didn't exempt me, however, from exhibiting a competitive hunger every time I received the green light to start a new project. God's amazing grace had made it possible for me to accomplish things that I never even contemplated, while also satisfying my heart's desire to pursue engineering.

In the early '80s, NCC qualified for HUD's Section 8 program by adding NC Commons Family, Gardens Family and Manor Family to its roster of family living low-income properties. Joseph Chieppa, a New Jersey housing finance official, was our longtime point person for the Section 8 program. More importantly, he was a leader when it came to developing housing for the poor. During this same time, the Prudential Insurance Company of America deeded its massive Douglass-Harrison apartment complex to NCC for one dollar. It was losing money on the heavily subsidized property. In a short matter of time, NCC had added over 1,000 units of housing to its growing stock. I believed the Section 8 program, which required tenants to pay 30 percent of their income for rent, offered a wonderful opportunity for people to aspire to do more with their lives. Tenants had the flexibility to enroll in college or other training programs since most of their rent was being subsidized by the federal government. And Section 8 could very well be a pathway to homeownership as well.

However, Mayor Gibson's non-profit housing agency posed a threat to the Newark Housing Authority, because of the government perks it was receiving to increase low-income housing. The Newark Housing Authority was still under the control of the old Addonizio regime, which caused the mayor tremendous anxiety. The roots of corruption ran deep in Newark and when Gibson took office, it was still risky business. Mob activity was high and many of the mayor's decisions were literally life and death choices.

But Gibson was buoyed by the fact that he was elected the first black mayor of a major northeastern city. He attracted a strong allegiance of black support from mainstream to Hollywood. I strongly believe the spirit of Black Nationalism, so right and ripe at the time, acted as a bulwark for him. Amiri Baraka was certainly a force in the city, and I think the mob thought twice about the repercussions if they tried to go after Gibson.

This "mandate" afforded Gibson the freedom he needed to move forward in the area of housing. Massaro responded by starting, "Newark's Neighborhood Improvement Program," offering homeowners an Urban Development Action Grant to spruce up the outside of their homes. Making them more weather efficient and aesthetically pleasing was the basis of the program.

Massaro managed to accrue $3.3 million in federal funds, with an additional $17 million invested in the program by eight community banks. The city backed 25 percent of the grant, while the banks involved in the program were obliged to grant the homeowner a loan for up to $40,000 against the equity in their property. The program had tremendous impact on what neighborhoods began to look like with the installation of aluminum siding and exterior paint jobs. Homeowners received free paint from the city and applying their own sweat equity was repayment enough for getting the job done.

This initiative allowed Gibson to bring the U. S. Secretary of Housing and Urban Development, Patricia Harris, the first black woman to serve in that post in President Jimmy Carter's administration, to Newark on more than one occasion. When Secretary Harris was in town, New Community was naturally included in Newark's showcase of housing development. We held elaborate groundbreaking ceremonies and dedications whenever we got the word that she was coming to town. NCC had a festive way of making the mayor shine. Newark's proximity to New York City – the shopping Mecca didn't hurt matters. Let me put it like this: we saw a lot of Secretary Harris.

Other U.S. Cabinet officials followed, such as Marcy Kaptur, the domestic policy advisor to President Carter. Now a congresswoman from Ohio, Marcy Kaptur would forgo the fancy hotels during her visits and lodge at St. Rose of Lima Rectory, where I had served as the pastor. I had a great deal of respect for her as a public servant and we became good friends.

The mayor had proven to be quite successful in getting Washington D.C. to focus on the plight of Newark. What New Community was accomplishing made Mayor Ken Gibson very proud, considering he was an original board member. More importantly, under his leadership, New Community had prospered and gained prominent recognition. Gibson and New Community were a winning combination.

However, all the good Mayor Gibson did for Newark was tarnished in a mayoral scandal. He eventually pleaded guilty to tax evasion. It was alleged that Gibson siphoned off $1 million from a contract that his firm received for a construction project in Irvington. Although he never served any jail time, he received probation and had to pay $349,000 in restitution.

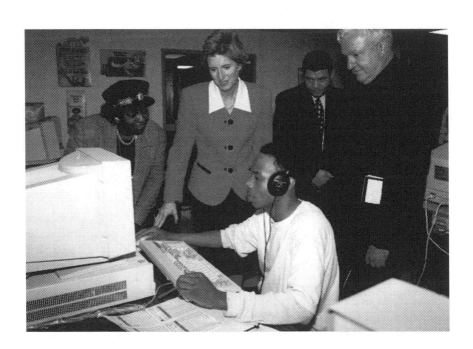

CHAPTER 17

NCC's Economic Stimulus: Pathmark Supermarket Shopping Center Comes to Newark

Give us today our daily bread - Matthew 6:11

Joe Chaneyfield and I were an anomaly. People just couldn't fathom a positive black and white relationship. Some whispered behind our backs, labeling Joe the "mean black guy" and me "the young white priest." Therefore, it was more acceptable for those who did not understand the concept of black and white people working together in harmony to refer to me as the "overseer." And at one point, Willie, of all people, was even labeled an "Uncle Tom."

The New Community Board of Directors were of a different breed and laughable among our faith-based competition that was wholly dependent on federal urban renewal funds. Since New Community chose to sidestep the political abyss of urban renewal money, we were never expected to get our projects funded.

After the '67 Summer Disorders, residents in the Central Ward had been unable to shop for the most essential items in their own community: food. All the small stores that had once populated Prince Street were destroyed in '67. Only 25 percent of the residents owned cars and so they were dependent on public transportation to do the family's grocery shopping.

Joe would take people by the busload every day up to Kearny and different places to buy food. It didn't make any sense. The money that was being spent in Kearny needed to be pumped into Newark instead. Besides, in many of these out-of-town locations, the residents of Newark were made to feel inferior because of their use of food stamps. The city's residents had once been in walking distance to those little shops, bakeries, a few blocks of small stores where they could buy fresh vegetables and other food items. That was all gone. In the meantime, people still needed to eat. The Central Ward needed a major grocery store.

Food was very personal to me, considering I had worked at the A&P when I was in high school. To have a supermarket in Newark, particularly in the Central Ward, was a part of the "new community" concept. Other surrounding cities, such as Elizabeth and Jersey City, as well as suburban towns, had access to large supermarkets. New Community had promoted making every aspect of living a good and decent life, accessible to the most vulnerable. Housing was just one component. However, if we could add a large supermarket to our child care, education, and health care models, it would set us apart from all other community development corporations. More importantly, it would create an economic engine for the community!

We had already identified the formula for "economic development" from the housing side of New Community. Seven or eight jobs were created for every 120 units of housing NCC produced. Each of our buildings required a manager, security force and one or more janitors. The need for a maintenance crew emerged and a robust management team followed to insure the integrity of various sites. It was now apparent that job creation was the direction in which we were headed.

This put the New Community brand in a spotlight that was attractive to politicians. Thomas Kean, during his first run for governor, brought his campaign to several of our senior citizen buildings, where public meetings were held. He asked the seniors: "What would you want the governor of New Jersey to do for you?"

"Get us a food store," was their unanimous response.

That was our starting point. We first did a survey of about 300 people and they picked out two chains that they wanted – Pathmark or ShopRite. Pathmark and its parent company, Supermarkets General, had a very good reputation, so I reached out to them on behalf of the board and the community. I kept missing the person I needed to talk to, Pathmark CEO Len Lieberman, and he kept missing me when he returned my call. Eventually though we connected. Governor Kean, in keeping with his campaign promise to our senior citizens, was very interested in the Pathmark deal. And Len Lieberman saw it as a way to make contact with the governor. Governor Kean arranged a meeting with Lieberman and I accompanied him to the meeting.

New Community was already one step ahead, because we owned the 60 lots that framed the corner of Bergen Street and South Orange Avenue, prime real estate location for the proposed project. The Pathmark deal was two-fold: it would give the community a major supermarket, which was sorely needed, while creating jobs. If we could get Pathmark, it would provide a sure economic boost to the Central Ward and for all those who laughed at us.

The joke was on them, because we were serious about making Pathmark a reality in Newark. It became one of our most important economic ventures. As it turned out, Pathmark wanted to come to Newark and was looking for an entity to partner with. However, before settling on New Community, representatives from Pathmark talked to a couple of people, one being Bob Curvin, another original board member of New Community. He advised the folks from Pathmark that we were the only group that could really pull this off. As the partnering entity, New Community would have two-thirds equity in the store that would flow back into the community. Pathmark wanted the assurance of security at the site because of the Newark location, which was understood.

NCC's Director of Development, Ray Codey, worked the deal. He negotiated with the city to lower the tax rates to make it enticing for Pathmark. A reduced tax bill over a period of 15 years would allow the business to flourish. Art Ryan, the CEO of Prudential Financial, signed on to help fund the $12 million dollar project. And James Kellogg, whom Governor Kean had appointed to the New Jersey Housing and Mortgage Finance Agency, was a tremendous help to us.

The CEO of Supermarkets General, Jack Futterman, led the team of individuals who worked diligently to get Pathmark up, operating and open. Of the close to 300 jobs that Pathmark would create, nearly half of them would be union jobs. That meant those employees would have full benefits and career oriented opportunities. They could rise to be department managers or general store managers. In addition, the 55,000-square-foot store would include a 1,000- square-foot pharmacy critical to the needs of the aging population in the Central Ward. We were good to go.

The nationwide fanfare, when the Pathmark Shopping Center opened its doors to the public on July 26, 1990, was a sight to behold. When Pathmark opened, Democratic Governor, James Florio was on hand, along with Newark Mayor Sharpe James and a host of other dignitaries. Speeches were made and even the mayor was on his best behavior. The shopping center also included a Dunkin Donuts and New Community-owned World of Foods, an idea that stemmed from my childhood, when my father would take the family out for a cultural dining experience. World of Foods would also create more jobs.

Pathmark was a major success. It was known for its fresh produce and seafood. We were able to incorporate health screenings in the store, which were vital to the needs of the community. The seniors were elated. Opening day at the Pathmark Shopping Center was pitch-perfect despite whatever else was happening in the city. The color of the day was joy and happiness and plenty of laughter.

CHAPTER 18

NCC "For Profit" Not Profitable

*For by grace you have been saved through faith, and this is
not from you; it is the gift of God* - Ephesians 2:8

The photo was dated October 1981 and showed me looking youthful while leading a tour of public officials around the grounds of New Community Commons Senior - a 222-unit residence for senior citizens. Called "A Look Back", the photo essay ran in the NCC *Clarion* newspaper. Included in the group of officials was Thomas Kean, before he was governor. Joe stood right behind me. Staring at the picture, I can still hear Joe's voice calling me, "Hey Padre." Joe always had my back.

When we first met, Joe had thought that I'd wilt after his invitation for me to join the men working on the sewer line at Queen of Angels. When I didn't, I gained his respect. He'd tell me: "Padre, I like your style." He was not a perfect person, but his good deeds were many. I was honored to call him my friend for nearly forty years. When Joe died in 2001, the ties that bound our friendship - love, trust and understanding - were severed. I was heartbroken. Joe was more than a friend; he was like the brother I never had.

Most people saw me as the face of New Community Corporation, but Joe was the "king" of the corporation. On any given night, you could find him sitting at the corner table at the World of Foods restaurant. A table was reserved especially for him and he held court there regularly. The manager of the restaurant didn't allow anyone to sit at "Joe's table." If there was a resident or employee of New Community who needed assistance, or if there was trouble brewing, the people went to see Joe at World of Foods. He listened intently and brought the matter to the proper person to resolve the problem.

Joe would go to war with someone who mistreated a woman or a child. He was a wide expanse of a man. And yet there he would be down on the floor at one of the Babyland day care centers playing with the children as if he was one of them. Joe was NCC's "Sergeant of Arms," so to speak, because he kept things in order. I remember him escorting a young lady home for a change of clothes after she'd been physically abused by her husband. And when hubby got flip at the lip with Joe. Lights out! Joe put him through a wall.

"Joe Chaneyfield Plaza" is a constant reminder to me of all the good things that Joe contributed to his community. It's not an everyday occasion that someone has a street named after them. The kids respected him. People like Craig Drinkard, now an adult and a successful professional, still remembers the lectures Joe preached to him and his buddies when they were growing up in New Community housing. Drinkard recalled some of the repercussions the kids faced when they didn't follow the rules.

"Mr. Chaneyfield used to tell us that we needed to respect where we lived and to take care of our community," said Drinkard. "Tyrone Bodison was served a $25 ticket by NCC security for walking on the grass. And boy was his momma mad."

Joe and I worked in tandem. I would come up with an idea and Joe saw to it that my vision came to life. Unfortunately, some of my ideas didn't pan out as I imagined they would. World of Foods is a great example. I envisioned a bi-level food court in the heart of Newark that would rival any suburban mall's food court and give patrons a cultural experience through food. Everything from barbecue, delicatessen selections, Mexican and Chinese would be served at World of Foods. With the success of Pathmark, I thought World of Foods would be a great addition to our shopping center, along with an NCC-acquired national Dunkin Donuts franchise.

World of Foods ended up bleeding the corporation of money like an unattended gunshot wound. Joe tried a different avenue to keep it going, hiring new management. That didn't work. It was a costly operation to run and even though New Community was not getting anything back on the return, my thing was that it was providing jobs. In some way I'm glad that Joe never saw its ultimate failure, as his death preceded the closing of World of Foods in 2004.

Yes, I confess my stubbornness has been a discerning flaw at times. Despite having studied at the prestigious Wharton School of Business's Executive Program, I often let my heart supersede my business acumen. Even when I was advised by Ray Codey, to get out of the restaurant business, I refused to budge. I was driven by the economic impact that our "for profit" investments could have on the community that I lost sight of the business component.

The idea of creating jobs was a high priority which led to St. Joseph Plaza. It included at one time a medical care office, a health spa, and a sandwich shop and conference center. But the Priory Restaurant and jazz club were the stars of the show in my mind. Although a swank restaurant and jazz club weren't all that appealing to the new generation of young people. Fine dining didn't seem to mix with the eruption of violence in Newark.

The Priory also became a major deficit in the loss category on our finance department's spreadsheet. Maintaining a full wait staff and paying them a minimum-wage salary plus tips was unheard of in the restaurant business. Add in the salary of a top chef recruited all the way from New Orleans and The Priory didn't make business sense. There just wasn't enough traffic to keep the restaurant running. In an effort to keep our feet in the business, an idea was raised to replace The Priory with "Sylvia's" Restaurant, the famous Harlem eatery. I turned that idea down. "Brothers" - a down home rib joint that was located on South Orange Avenue for years was also discussed. That idea never went anywhere either and The Priory Restaurant was eventually shut down.

Unfortunately, the Priory wasn't the only problem we had to contend with. There was the failure of the New Community Corporation Print Shop. It never generated the corporate clientele we'd hoped for. Having to rely on printing wedding and birthday invitations just wasn't enough to make it a worthwhile enterprise. Dunkin Donuts at the Pathmark Shopping Center, initially profitable, became another unstoppable bleeding wound after a management change. We were losing money by the hundreds of thousands of dollars.

Talk about growing pains—we were feeling them. Housing was our most stable commodity and it was starting to suffer as a result of the "for profits" draining the corporation of money. During the '80s and '90s, New Community had grown exponentially. By 1999, we owned 19 housing development properties totaling close to 3,000 units that were located in Newark's Central and West Wards, Jersey City and Englewood. That was at the height of NCC's business, when we employed 2,300 people and were one of Newark's largest employers. The reins at New Community had to be tightened so that the corporation could sustain itself and run more efficiently. That meant we had to scale back our workforce, which of course, was tough for me, because New Community was in the business of hiring people and giving them jobs, not taking them away.

But matters got progressively worse and by 2007 NCC had entered some murky waters. We had to do more than cut our payroll. We began to downsize and sold two-thirds of our interest in the Pathmark operation. We'd started receiving negative press, lambasted in the media for not paying our Public Service Electric and Gas bill. A headline in the *Star-Ledger* read: "Monsignor Wiliam Linder: Q &A with head of Newark's troubled New Community Corp." New Community had owed PSE&G over a million dollars.

In that interview with the *Star-Ledger* I clearly told the reporter, "We have other things, such as the services at Harmony House. We get some federal aid for day care, which always runs seriously in the red. But if you ask me whether I'll pay the teacher at Harmony House or PSE&G, it's the teacher who'll get paid."

Nevertheless, we still needed to find a way to stop the hemorrhaging of our money. Hope seemed to be all that was left. And it came in the form of an apartment complex called Stony Hill, located in Eatontown, down near the Jersey shore. Prior to our financial problems, Ray had worked a deal with Carteret Savings and Loan that allowed us to purchase the apartment complex in a dispersal sale for $10,000 cash down. The bank was bankrupt and was looking to unload the property.

And, along with the cash payment, we'd secured a $600,000 loan from the Housing and Mortgage Finance Agency to complete the sale with Carteret Savings and Loan.

I authorized Ray to sell the property. I was not fond of selling land, but Eatontown was way out of NCC's jurisdiction and maintaining the property had become a hassle. Ray set up a competitive auction for the sale of the apartment complex and New Community received $9 million from the sale. After we paid off the $600,000 loan from the Housing Mortgage Finance Agency, we profited enough to pay off NCC's debt to PSE&G, as well as other looming financial obligations. I was grateful to Ray for making a deal that helped NCC regain its financial equilibrium.

Those were some of the growing pains that we had to deal with while trying to be all things to the community. Nevertheless, New Community emerged stronger, wiser and more efficient as a corporation. And today, though NCC's workforce is trimmed to 600 employees, as a result of severing ties with Babyland and Pathmark, our average minimum-wage employee is paid $11 an hour.

PART III

NCC Gains National Prominence

CHAPTER 19

Hope: The Most Spontaneous Prayer There Is

May the God of hope fill you with all joy and peace in believing, so that you may abound in hope by the power of the holy Spirit - Romans 15:13

With the creation of the Pathmark Shopping Center it garnered New Community national attention, causing the telephone to start jumping off the hook. Representatives from community development corporations from across the nation wanted to visit our offices.

In 1991, my focus was on the arts because of their importance to the NCC community-building plan. When I discovered that an arts and economic development conference would be taking place in Chicago, I made plans to attend. I knew the arts were transformative for those who participated in them, as well as those who simply experienced them. I wasn't the only one who felt this way.

William Strickland, the founder of the Manchester Craftsmen's Guild, better known as MCG Jazz, had been devoted to preserving, presenting and promoting jazz in Pittsburgh, Pennsylvania, since 1987. A jazz lover like me, Strickland was also the CEO of Manchester Bidwell Corporation, a CDC dedicated to offering vocational training to displaced and underemployed workers. I had tremendous respect for what Strickland was doing in Pittsburgh - building community partnerships that provided a brighter tomorrow for those in need.

The conference in Chicago was sponsored by the MacArthur Foundation. When I called to inquire about the event, I was told that I could not attend. It seemed as though they were inviting specific people and organizations that were more artistically inclined. A community development corporation such as New Community seemingly didn't fit the bill. To persuade them to let me attend, I offered to pay for my own travel expenses. I was desperate to find out what we could do at New Community to enhance our community arts focus. I was told no again.

Soon thereafter, I received a message that someone from the MacArthur Foundation had called. I immediately returned the call, certain that they'd had a change of heart because of my persistence.

"Hi this is Monsignor William Linder returning your call," I said.

"Thanks for getting back to me," said the representative on the line. "Congratulations. You've just been awarded a MacArthur Fellowship."

"I don't want a fellowship," I replied curtly. "All I want is to attend your conference on the arts and economic development." The representative on the line started laughing. Then he proceeded to tell me what being chosen as a MacArthur Fellow meant: Receiving a $330,000 grant that would be paid to me in installments over the next five years. That was pretty incredible considering I'd only wanted to go to an arts conference. As it turned out, Bill Strickland had also been the recipient of the MacArthur Fellowship "genius" award.

My MacArthur Fellowship fortuitously served to establish New Community as a viable and credible entity. Doors that were previously closed suddenly opened in the worlds of business and government. We began to attract other philanthropic foundations. Half of the money I received went toward scholarships for the corporation's children's endowment fund. I used about $10,000 of the money from the fellowship to live on and used some of the rest for travel expenses.

My invitations to make speeches about community development had doubled since Pathmark Shopping Center had opened. Thanks to the fellowship, I was able to accept more invitations without them being a financial liability to New Community. I never felt that these community groups should have to pay my way to talk to them. Prior to being awarded the MacArthur Fellowship, New Community had always paid my travel expenses, as most of these community groups couldn't afford to. They could just barely hustle up an honorarium for me that went directly back to NCC. Being the recipient of the fellowship removed this burden from the corporation.

What more could I expect after the MacArthur Fellowship? It had seemed to be the icing on the cake. But then one day I received a telephone call, this one from the national office of Catholic Charities. It was during the time Bill Clinton was first campaigning for president. The person on the other end of the telephone wanted to know if we could accommodate Hillary Clinton, who wanted to visit a day care center and speak to some teenage mothers.

"Can we accommodate Hillary Clinton?" I responded in shock. "Of course we can." I was then informed that Mrs. Clinton was not intending for this to be a campaign stop. She planned to talk to the press about programs such as our Babyland III location on South Orange Avenue, where teen mothers took parenting classes while their children were cared for in a nurturing environment. These young mothers did not have to compromise their education, because they knew their children were in good hands.

The Secret Service arrived a week ahead of Mrs. Clinton. The day of her visit on September 15, 1992, all the local and state politicians were on hand to greet her. When it came time to meet with the teen mothers, Mrs. Clinton asked the political officials to excuse themselves from the room. I, along with Mary Smith, the director of all seven of our Babyland Nurseries, Senator Frank Lautenberg and Congressman Donald Payne Sr. were the only people allowed to remain in the room.

After her visit with the young mothers, Mrs. Clinton then toured the Babyland facility. The media caught up with her in the courtyard but every time they tried to engage her with a question about her husband's campaign, she politely said, "No, I'm not here for that." It was obvious that the reporters weren't too interested in the issues of teenage pregnancy or what happens to the children afterward. Mrs. Clinton visited with us for about two hours and then got into her car and left.

A couple of months after Mrs. Clinton's visit, Bill Clinton was elected as president in November of 1992. Shortly after that I received yet another telephone call.

"Were you the Monsignor who greeted Mrs. Clinton at the entrance of Babyland III?" The Whitehouse aide asked.

"Yes," I said.

"Well, Mrs. Clinton would like to invite you to be her guest at the upcoming Presidential Inauguration (January 20, 1993), as one of the Faces of Hope." My jaw dropped. President-elect Bill Clinton and Mrs. Clinton, along with Vice-President-elect Al Gore and Mrs. Gore, had hand-picked people they had met along the campaign trail and in their other travels. I was humbled that such an honor had come my way.

I spent a week being treated like royalty in Washington, D.C., along with the other Faces of Hope. The White House hosted a luncheon for us where I was seated next to Mrs. Clinton. While much of the conversation at the luncheon centered on small-business development. Mrs. Clinton had been well briefed about the people who were at the luncheon. She knew all about the work we were doing in our communities. From that day on, my admiration for Hillary Clinton grew stronger. And although she lost the 2008 presidential Democratic primary race to Barack Obama, I voted for her. However, I'm hoping her bid for the 2016 Presidential election works out in her favor. I had never imagined an African American being elected president in my lifetime. So I'm enthused to vote for Hillary Clinton again, considering she could become the first woman president of the United States.

Over the years, what I've come to understand is that anything is possible in life. That certainly is what I felt when I received the invitation to attend Bill Clinton's Presidential Inauguration. That was symbolic for me, because the year 1993 marked the 25th anniversary of New Community Corporation - from a mustard seed of an idea to New Jersey's largest non-profit community development corporation - garnering national prominence. I was as pleased as a proud parent with the continuing growth of New Community.

That same year was also significant because it marked my 57th birthday. My colleagues at New Community threw me a surprise party. My mother was there reveling in the jubilant atmosphere, dancing the night away. It would be the last image I have of my mother alive. She died that very night in her sleep. She had disclosed to me right before her death that she wanted to go home to see her husband. Naturally, I was shocked by her death but when I had a moment to consider my mother's desire I thought, *What better way to go.*

Meanwhile, good fortune continued to flow in New Community's direction. Armed with a solid portfolio of real estate, we played an important role in Newark's revitalization. So when the application for the federally-funded Hope I Grant for $25 million dollars was made public, I was confident that we had a good shot at getting it. However, we applied and were denied. We filed an appeal, but did not win. I strongly believed that we deserved the grant and thus could not accept "no" for an answer.

My stubbornness led to New Jersey Senator Bill Bradley's involvement. He reached out to Henry Cisneros, secretary of the U.S. Department of Housing and Urban Development under President Bill Clinton. I traveled to Washington, D.C., and met with Secretary Cisneros and Senator Bradley. Senator Bradley asked the Secretary to come to Newark so that he could see for himself what New Community was all about. Secretary Cisneros and his wife accepted Bradley's offer and came to Newark. We extended them the full tour of New Community. By 1993, we housed nearly 6,000 residents in more 2,500 units of housing in Newark that was attractive, safe and affordable. The Secretary appeared to be quite impressed with our comprehensive approach to community-building. We offered services that addressed every stage of life, from transitional housing for homeless families at Harmony House, Babyland early childhood education, vocational training through our Workforce Development Center and our Extended Care nursing home facility for seniors and disabled adults.

The tour ended with Secretary Cisneros getting an eyeful of the realities of public housing. We ran smack into a drug deal when we ventured into one of the public housing properties. Even in the midst of strangers, the dealer and buyer never stopped the transaction or tried to conceal what they were doing. Secretary Cisneros didn't seem unnerved by what was happening. Once we got outside, however, he said it was outrageous that someone could walk into public housing and be greeted by such a profane act.

"Welcome to public housing," I told him. Drug deals were the reality and a way of life for so many residents. Before departing, Secretary Cisneros told us that he was headed to Washington, D. C., and that he was going to award New Community the Hope I Grant after all.

The grant led to the construction of Community Hills in 1995: 206 townhomes built for first-time homebuyers located on Irvine Turner Boulevard. About 30 foster parents were among those vying for the townhomes. I strongly believed that it was a way for them to continue to provide an even more stable environment for the children in their care. Community Hills was staffed with a 24-hour security guard and an extra feature for the families included an onsite day care facility.

Hope has been the one constant in my life. It's the most spontaneous prayer there is. New Community was the first and last recipient of the Hope I Grant. The MacArthur Fellowship and the Faces of Hope distinction was God's answer to my prayer for hope.

MONSIGNOR WILLIAM J. LINDER

CHAPTER 20

NCC: A Global Missionary

He said to them, "Go into the whole world and proclaim the gospel to every creature" - Mark 16:15

My mission for the last 50 years has been to serve God's people. I feel truly blessed that New Community Corporation celebrated its 48th Anniversary in March of 2016. I still receive invitations from far-flung places to come and speak about community and economic development. One invitation came from a delegation that was traveling to Cuba in 2012. Although my mind was ready, willing and able, I had to decline the invite because my body said, "no way."

The missionary work I completed during my pastoral tenure at St. Rose of Lima Church in the Roseville section of Newark, from 1974 until I retired in 2012, was unprecedented. St. Rose of Lima allowed for an interesting mix of ideas and experiences, unlike Queen of Angels, which was predominantly an all-black parish. St. Rose of Lima represented 40 countries across the globe. The multi-ethnic mix of people at St. Rose of Lima created a "foreign exchange" agenda for New Community.

The agenda extended its roots back to 1973 when I visited Cuernavaca, Mexico, to spend an entire summer at the *Centro Intercultural de Documentacion* Center. I was there to study the languages and cultures of South America. It was one of the best courses I had ever enrolled in. The school was founded by Ivan Illich, a philosopher and radical Roman Catholic priest. Throughout my life I've always been attracted to radicalism and taken pride in wearing it like a badge of honor. However, what I learned from that cultural immersion was how native Mexicans blended the social and religious, which was also what New Community aimed to do.

There have been times when I've been absolutely astounded by the invocation of the combination of the religious and the social operating together as a change agent. But I've always seen community development as a religious activity. With the success of the Pathmark Shopping Center during the '90s, New Community became a revolving door for international visitors.

That was the case when representatives from the state of Lagos, Nigeria, came to see me at St. Rose of Lima. They were interested in creating an economic development program that would bring Nigerian nurses to America. The salary they would receive here would support nine family members back home. In addition to that, approximately 30 women, some from Nigeria and other areas in East Africa, followed and were enrolled in New Community's Licensed Practical Nursing program.

With a population of close to 10 million people, the African student exchange from Lagos that we linked with our nursing program was quite significant, considering what poverty looks like in Nigeria as compared with America. Sixty-three percent of the country lives on less than one dollar a day. In response, we created a program with a dual nature. Not only would Africa benefit economically from the exchange, but New Community would as well. I had witnessed for myself the compassion that African people had for their elderly during my travels in the early '70s. That kind of compassion fit perfectly with New Community's Extended Care Facility.

Today, Nigerian native Veronica Onwunaka is the director of nursing at our Extended Care Facility. It is shameful that American culture only finds value in what's young. And at all costs, for those who spend ungodly sums of money trying to hold onto a time that has come and gone, they could support an entire African nation.

In the mid-'90s, I had the opportunity to travel to the Baltic region of Northern Europe. In Latvia and Estonia there was no concept of the church's role in community development. The churches there were made to be politically weak. My first lecture centered on the published works titled, "An Alternative Community Development Model in Religious Context" and "Neighborhood Development in Context." I had collaborated with my mentor and friend, Dr. Gerald Shattuck, on these works that centered on the three inter-related and indispensable dimensions of religion that were at work in the area of community development: religion as community, religion as vision and religion as empowerment.

I expressed the importance of the church assessing and identifying certain things about the community. Who are we? What is the personality and character of the community? As a visionary, the church had to ask: Where are we going? What is the potential of this community? The church needed to be the most empowering and imposing entity there was outside of the political realm in all communities. The church should empower a community by asking: How will the strategic design and model be fulfilled? The churches in Northern Europe needed to grasp these dynamics in order to become an enterprising force in community development.

Like Jesus said: "As you sent me into the world, so I *sent* them into the world." (John 17:18). I've always seen New Community as part of a missionary movement.

We raised a few eyebrows when a delegation from Poland arrived. They were amazed to see St. Rose of Lima functioning in an egalitarian way with businesses, financial institutions and philanthropic foundations such as the Ford Foundation all under one umbrella supporting one common goal, a civil society. They marveled at the workshops they attended, where 85 percent of the people facilitating and teaching them were black. In addition to our community development, we also brought the issue of race to the forefront, including people who were often oppressed in this country, into our operation.

Surprisingly, the feature that fascinated our international audience most was how New Community maneuvered as a corporation, while avoiding ties to the capricious nature of local government. Clearly that was exposed when the China and the Soviet delegations showed up on the doorstep at St. Rose of Lima. Everything with both delegations was political. The self-sufficient infrastructure of New Community was hard for them to fathom.

The overall concept for New Community today starts with close to 2,000 units of family and senior citizen housing. Employment is critical to our self-sufficient model and the corporation itself employs 600 people. Others can access employment opportunities throughout the city and surrounding areas at our Family Resource Success Center, located at the former Pathmark Shopping Center. Equally important are those Newark residents, who otherwise cannot access community college and thus find an alternative route through our vocational education at our "Workforce Development Center." They're the poorest of the poor, deprived of all hopes and dreams. In some parts of the world, they're known as the "street" people or the "untouchables." In some cases these individuals may not even have an address. Homeless. New Community also provides transitional housing for them at Harmony House. Living in a more stable environment and having access to gainful employment, residents can have their banking needs met at the New Community Federal Credit Union and work toward establishing credit. And all the "good" news that they want to read can be found in the monthly *Clarion* newspaper, which is distributed to 15,000 readers in the NCC network and across the U.S. We give families access to affordable child care and our seniors, who we consider as vital to the community, are administered heavy doses of dignity and respect at our Extended Care Facility.

New Community Corporation continues to meet all the vital needs of the family unit and the collective community. It is the measurement of success that has set NCC apart from all other community development corporations. "From the cradle to the grave," we believe that New Community has got it covered

The many international anchors dropped in the sea of humanity by New Community led me to travel extensively. I've been to Ireland 14 times. I was on their board for the Children's Friendship Project until 2007. We've done good work in Ireland because of the benefit of a mutual relationship. It started in 1998 with the women's conference titled "Vital Voices," held in Belfast, Ireland. There I reunited with my good friend, Hillary Clinton. She was there to deliver the keynote address and I was leading a workshop on community development and economics. When the director of the conference started to introduce me to Mrs. Clinton she said: "Oh, the Monsignor and I are old friends." Her speech centered on women's economic progress being vital to the Democratic process. It was a dynamic conference. Prior to her address in Belfast, Hillary had asserted at the World Conference on Women in Beijing, China, that "Women's rights are human rights and human rights are women's rights." Despite what people may say about Hillary Clinton, her advocacy for women and children has never wavered.

Meanwhile, the result of my work at the women's conference led to a number of delegations from Ireland coming to Newark. A group of 12 that came and spent a week at New Community in 1999 made for a particularly memorable occasion. The highlight of the trip was the send-off of one particular delegation. They mainly hailed from Northern Ireland, Protestant territory. And at that time, our Director of Development, Ray Codey, and his wife, Peggy, were gracious enough to host a number of dinner parties at their home in Chatham. This particular delegation included Catholics and citizens from Southern Ireland.

The party got off to a rocky start due to the tensions between the Protestants and Catholics. I recall two members of the delegation, one Protestant from Northern Ireland, meeting with an Irish Catholic. As it turned out, they knew each other quite well; one had shot the other during the turbulent times in Ireland. Despite that, they bonded as friends and were actually hugging each other at the party's conclusion as they prepared to return back home.

When petty differences of religion and race are set aside, we can all have fun together, as we did that evening at Ray and Peggy's home. Irish Protestants and Catholics dancing and singing together in harmony ... it was one wild night!

MONSIGNOR WILLIAM J. LINDER

MONSIGNOR WILLIAM J. LINDER

CHAPTER 21

Not the Sharper Image

Whatever you do, do from the heart, as for the Lord and not for others, knowing that you will receive from the Lord the due payment of the inheritance; be slaves of the Lord Christ. For the wrongdoer will receive recompense for the wrong he committed, and there is no partiality – Colossians 3:23-25

One of the first things Mayor Sharpe James did once he was elected in 1986 was visit us at New Community to pledge his support. That was really good for us, especially since we had worked so well with the Gibson administration. However, once Mayor Sharpe James took office, the love relationship between New Community and City Hall took a turn for the worse. By then, NCC was well established when it came to low-income housing developments. While New Community was focused on building housing for those in need, it became evident that Mayor James' priority was elsewhere.

The New Jersey Performing Arts Center (NJPAC) was first proposed in 1986 and touted as the cornerstone of the "Newark Renaissance." The intoxicating buzz for this proposed "diamond" that would save Newark from itself and bring it back from the brink of destruction was nothing more than window dressing. With the rising homeless situation happening in Newark, I was totally opposed to the project. My thoughts were aligned with those of the U.S. Catholic bishops: "Human dignity can be realized and protected only in community."

Whose human dignity was James protecting in the community? His focus was light years away from Newark's growing problem – the homeless and the rising population of people stricken with HIV/AIDS. Were these human beings exempt from being treated with dignity? The mayor seemed largely unfazed by the epidemic though he did appoint Richard Powell as the city's AIDS czar in 1989. This was during the time when Babyland was still associated with New Community and had opened one of the nation's first day care centers for children infected with HIV at that time.

My fanaticism for ministering to the homeless was infused with shots of Liberation Theology - an understanding that Christians are entrusted to support the weak and poor. Social change was at the crux of the theology and the words of Father Jon Sobrino focused my attention in dealing with this issue. "Give a new form to a now wretched reality." Nothing was more wretched, to me, than a person who had nowhere to live. A mother battered by an abusive spouse and her children, through no fault of their own, lost and turned out in the cold. Others in high places seemed to accept these things. I could not.

New Community owned an empty parcel of land adjacent to our 180-bed Extended Care Facility, which not only served the frail and elderly, but also created approximately 250 jobs. The facility was the first of its kind to be Medicaid eligible in Newark. However, the land it was built upon was insured by HUD, with which NCC had an agreement. In order to break ground on transitional housing for the homeless, we had to get a release of land from HUD. The matter was urgent. And when federal housing officials proved to be slow in issuing New Community the permit, I called HUD Secretary Jack Kemp's office directly. In less than 30 minutes, I received the release for the land in question so construction could begin on Harmony House, our 102-unit transitional residence with a daycare facility on site. It was a surreal moment, because I hardly expected the release to be issued that quickly. It was clear to me - New Community had earned a reputation as a well-respected and solid corporation.

The advancing footprint of New Community was something to behold. The corporation's green and white Etch-a-Sketch house logo seemed to be dancing all along the 14th Avenue and Hayes Street corridors in the Central Ward. New Community was more visible than ever before in the Central Ward. And now we were about to give hope to someone in their darkest hour. Everything it took to get to that moment was worth it.

Harmony House was completed in December 1989 and was ready for occupancy just in time for the holidays. There was just one problem: We hadn't been granted a certificate of occupancy from City Hall. There's no doubt in my mind that it had everything to do with my outspoken opposition to James' NJPAC project. He was playing to a totally different audience than mine and it certainly wasn't the homeless population.

However, without a certificate of occupancy, those in desperate need of a place to live were not only being denied shelter but access to an on-site day care facility, vocational training and employment assistance.

Luckily, divine intervention showed up in the form of a Channel 7 Eyewitness News reporter eager to do a story on Harmony House. She toured the facility and thought everything was beautiful. I told her we had not received a certificate of occupancy from City Hall. She then asked: "Do you mind if I take that situation up with City Hall?"

"No not at all. Please do," I said.

She went down to City Hall and was actually able to see the mayor. She told him in so many words: "Look, Christmas is coming and we have a Christmas tree in the middle courtyard and we're going to light it up. Channel 7 is going to cover it. You have a choice. We're either going to talk about the homeless having occupancy and you can light up the Christmas tree, or you can be Scrooge. You're going to be on TV, like it or not." After that we received the certificate.

In my opinion, James was always more concerned about what was going on downtown than anywhere else in a city where its neighborhoods were in dire need. And during his tenure as mayor (1986-2006), I did not mince my criticism about his priorities when it came to addressing the needs of poor people in Newark. His retaliation against New Community, aimed directly at me, meant we were denied two federal block grants, one in the amount of $35,000 and another one for $100,000.

Although I did receive the key to the city in 1991, I am convinced it had everything to do with us partnering with Supermarket General to bring Pathmark to Newark. That deal made the mayor look good. The feted gesture by the city had very little bearing on me, because I see no real connection between awards and the value of actual work. In fact, upon Mayor James' last inaugural celebration, before the scandal hit, he'd stood before a crowd of more than 1,000 people and announced at the Robert Treat Hotel that I was his worst enemy. I felt proud to be a topic of discussion at such a festive occasion. I guess you could say I earned it. I've never been impressed by pomp and circumstance, but rather by the good deeds of people. In the case of the 35th mayor of Newark, his "good" deeds were known to a certain few.

The success of Pathmark and its effect on the community led me to believe that New Community could do even more. My vision for the Central Ward was in overdrive. We owned a small parcel of land not far from Pathmark close in proximity to, what was then, the University of Medicine and Dentistry of New Jersey. In an effort to continue stimulating that part of the Central Ward, we came up with an idea to partner with the state to build an administrative building. After all, Pathmark was a testament to what was possible.

This project with the state would create clerical entry-level positions and management opportunities for qualifying Central Ward residents. The state's visibility in the community would be an asset. With that said, Ray was instrumental in drawing up a plan that also included a housing complex, for UMDNJ resident students. Prudential was on board to help with the funding and UMDNJ was in agreement along with the state. In other words, all cylinders were firing a resounding "yes" for the project.

The artistic rendering for the project was drawn up with the affixed "NCC" green and white logo and given to City Hall for its approval, along with letters of approval from the state and UMDNJ. Three weeks after the rendering was submitted, George Branch, who was the Central Ward councilman at the time, called the New Community offices trying desperately to get a hold of me. I was not available. By the time I read the message it said: "Get down to City Hall right away. Your proposed project is being presented before council." Was I too late?

Happily, I was informed by another staff member that Ray had gone in my place. After all, he'd worked closely on the project.

When Ray walked into Council Chambers down at City Hall, there was our project rendering on display. The shocking truth was that the NCC logo had been removed and replaced with an unfamiliar logo that read, "WKA Development." As it turned out, the mayor had shopped our project to Wilbert Allen, a representative of WKA Developers and the plan was to condemn a portion of the lots that belonged to NCC, through eminent domain and for the city to take over and do the project.

When Ray finally got a hold of me and informed me about what was happening, it was like something out of Shakespeare's Macbeth, a display of greed and power run amuck. The tragedy in all of this was that it revealed that James was not a man of integrity. No matter what I felt about the mayor, I tended to believe that there was a modicum of decency about the man. I was wrong. What ensued afterward was irrelevant, but the project never materialized

In 1997, NJPAC became a reality but at whose expense? The lineage of corruption that has historically plagued Newark continued under James. James' arrogance and vindictive ways eventually got in his way and led to his conviction on five counts of fraud in April of 2008. His time served in federal prison is not going to cure the malignant cancer of corruption that has existed here in Newark for so long, however. Former Newark Mayor, Cory Booker, now a United States senator, was more politically savvy than his predecessors. He exited the mayoral office unscathed by the corrosive disease of corruption for which Newark has become notorious. As with Addonizio, who had full support of the people, particularly the black leaders in the community, even after he was indicted, convicted and sentenced, so did James.

MONSIGNOR WILLIAM J. LINDER

CHAPTER 22

The End of an Era

They that hope in the Lord will renew their strength, they will soar on eagles' wings; They will run and not grow weary, walk and not grow faint – Isaiah 40:31

It took a decade of holding meetings, planning and, finally, building to develop New Community Homes Court, the first property owned by New Community Corporation, in 1975. And so it hurt to see it reduced to mere rubble in less than a week, more than four decades later, when it was demolished in 2010. There was no visible sign of all the painstaking hard work and effort that had gone into getting those six buildings erected. The structural quality of Homes Court had been first-rate. It truly was a sorrowful occasion, as if someone close to me had died. Many of the original residents of Homes Court were by then deceased. The property's time had come and gone.

As the demolition dust swirled, my thoughts raced to the building's first residents, such as Ms. Lola Stewart. Her watchful eyes from the third floor balcony warded off all foolishness and protected the children playing in the courtyard. During warmer months, open-air musical concerts filled the courtyard with music and laughter. The sense of ownership among the early tenants made Homes Court not only a safe residential complex, but a tightly-knit community. Many tenants had moved from cold water flats or dilapidated housing. Having the opportunity to move into a brand-new apartment that tenants helped to create engendered a tremendous source of pride. However, with each subsequent generation that moved into Homes Court, the initial neighborhood pride eroded, until it became utterly irrelevant. Then, things turned ugly.

What followed became grist for the anti-William Linder mill. New Community fended off media reports that cast us in a negative light. An unauthorized video shot at one of the apartments insinuated that we were a bad landlord.

Prior to the demolition of New Community Homes Court and the Douglass-Harrison complex, which fell victim to rampant drug dealing, we had been vigilant in reorganizing New Community's property management division. As New Community grew, some areas of its management and operations suffered. Looking forward, NCC is committed to strengthening our property management division. In fact, there is now a property manager at every site. There's also an asset manager, who keeps close tabs on the physical condition of the property to ensure that the site is in compliance with local ordinances, and state and federal guidelines. New Community's director of property management has implemented a housing committee comprising representatives from every area involved with housing – from the environmental staff to social service workers. The group has committed to meet twice a month to discuss and exchange information to help maintain properties at the highest level.

New Community has always put the dignity of people first, no matter their social status. In 2013, the average annual income of a resident living in NCC housing was less than $13,000. Ninety-five percent of the children who attended the former Newton Street School, which now houses an alternative high school program, meet the eligibility requirement to receive free lunch and most of them live in New Community housing. Craig Drinkard, who grew up at New Community Gardens Family townhomes on 14th Avenue, said that he never knew he lived in low-income housing because it was so nice. That's the meaning of dignity. Low income should not be synonymous with degradation. No one should be trapped into believing that they are lesser because of where they live. The poor deserve to have their needs met just the same as a well-to-do individual.

We cater specifically to the needs of the most vulnerable in society – seniors and children. Our Extended Care Facility's dementia and Alzheimer's care provides equally vital services to the lives of our older residents as the early learning centers do for children. For many years, the nursing home's adult medical daycare program provided our seniors with transportation to their doctor's appointments and engaged them in activities and trips that enriched their lives. The program eventually wound down and was replaced by the nursing home's specialization in dementia and Alzheimer treatment, which is a taboo topic in the black community.

As NCC moves forward as a corporation, it will continue to be a beacon of hope for those who have lost their way or are simply in need. The thing that I am most proud of is that NCC is not a "hand-out." We provide opportunities for people to better their lives. That's how you make a difference.

CHAPTER 23

A Legacy of Education

Hold fast to instruction, never let it go; keep it, for it is your life – Proverbs 4:13

In the words of Frederick Douglass, "It is easier to build strong children than to repair broken men." With that quote in mind, I established my namesake scholarship fund over 30 years ago to help students access the best education available. Young people are our best commodity for a promising future. If we do not invest in them in ways that encourage, enrich and engage all of who they are then there is little hope for the future.

Since its inception, the Monsignor William J. Linder Scholarship has provided over 2,000 scholarships to high school and college bound students. New Community's annual Spring Festival, held at the New Community Neighborhood Center, affords us with the opportunity to publicly uplift our young people while presenting them with the money to attend a reputable grammar, high school or boarding school of their choice.

The backdrop of the festival has always served as a joyous occasion for the student presentations, but the 2012 spring festival left me in a reflective mood. By providing these young people with the audacity to dream we moved them beyond a world of drugs, violence and mayhem. That year's crop of scholars were on the precipice of discovering a world bigger than the one they came from. In fact, I'm sure I felt my heart pitter-patter and fill with hopeful emotion of a brighter tomorrow. It's not often that I take the time to smell the roses, but this was one of those moments.

Indeed, it was worthy of a celebration. I recall the DJ putting on

Poppa Was a Rollin' Stone, by the Temptations kicking off the senior citizens dance contest. Besides the scholarship presentations, that was another highlight of the evening. Approximately 10 seniors, ranging in ages from 62 to 90, lined up to get their chance on the dance floor. It was something to see and as I took it all in - the crowd, the raffling off of gift prizes, and a cultural smorgasbord of rice and beans, collard greens and all the fixings - a moment of clarity washed over me. *They know what it feels like to have dignity,* I thought as I scanned the room filled with close to 300 people from the community. The previous 50 years of my life had been devoted for moments just like this: "To help residents of inner cities improve the quality of their lives to reflect individual God-given dignity and personal achievement." This guiding mission statement has governed New Community Corporation for all these years. For me to witness it in full force was breathtaking.

The roar of the crowd redirected my attention back onto the dance floor where Agnes Hughes, a spry 78-year-old senior from New Community Manor Senior Housing, was conjuring up dance moves to Michael Jackson's "Beat It" that would put a 20-something-year-old to shame. I couldn't help but to chuckle. And as it turned out, Agnes was named the undisputed senior citizen dance contest winner for 2012. She received a much deserved standing ovation. That night was a blessing.

Following the senior dance contest, 17-year-old Suzanne Ramsahai gave a speech as the recipient of the Monsignor Linder Scholarship Award. A student at Immaculate Conception High School in Montclair, Suzanne graduated in June 2012 and was accepted to LaSalle University in Philadelphia, where she graduated in 2016 with her bachelor's in psychology. Another scholar, Francesca Temitope Olufemi, attended Saint Vincent Academy in Newark through the scholarship fund, where Sister June Favata, a dear friend of mine, has been an administrator for 42 years, educating young urban women from Newark and surrounding areas. Olufemi was also accepted to Penn State University in the fall of 2012. They are just two out of the group of students who excelled at their respective high schools and have now enrolled in some of the nation's most prestigious universities: Harvard, Princeton, Rutgers, Georgetown and Loyola to name a few.

From the upstart of Babyland, in the early days until now with the William J. Linder Scholarship program, NCC has always taken education very seriously. In 2001 NCC's Community Hills Early Learning Center opened, providing pre-school education and childcare for three-and-four-year-olds. At that impressionable age, instilling and stimulating the love of learning in children is crucial.

However, it takes dynamic people to make that happen. And NCC is fortunate to have Nyonontee Jackman as such a person. She has taught at our Community Hills center since 2008. What an honor it was for her to be selected as the 2013 "Preschool Teacher of the Year," by the Newark Office of Early Childhood Education. In accepting the award, Jackman said it best: "I do this just knowing that one day I am going to see these kids as adults and they are going to be doctors and lawyers and teachers, and I will know that I had a part in giving them a love of education."

A good quality education provides the foundation for a good quality life. School choice is something I believe in, because the value of education and its creative coefficient on both the student and teacher's part is virtually nonexistent in today's public schools. Parents need to have a choice as to where they send their children to school. And through the scholarship fund, students ready to enter high school have been able to attend good quality schools.

NCC helped to establish New Horizons Community Charter School in 1999 for kindergarten through fifth grade, and then Lady Liberty Academy Charter School in 2001 for grades K-7. New Community also purchased the building for North Star Academy Charter School. We were in the position to buy the building for the school when it started in 1997, and we later sold the building to the school when they were financially able to purchase it. Although we're no longer involved with the daily operations at any of these schools, we're proud to have introduced other alternatives to the traditional public school education.

I challenged the archdiocese when I was at Queen of Angels to provide all students with access to a parochial education, whether they were Catholic or not. The same applied when I was transferred to St. Rose of Lima Church. In 1975, Art Wilson, a long-time parishioner at Queen of Angels and former NCC board member, was appointed principal of St. Rose of Lima Catholic School. He was the first lay principal of the school and served there for 34 years. He and the staff were dedicated to the students. They extended a quality education to predominately black and Latino students from the Roseville section of Newark, and increased the academic success of the K-8 student body.

But the fact remained that most families could not afford to pay the tuition any longer, largely due to the lack of jobs and prevailing low-income wages. Many of the students, who remained at the school, were able to do so because they were receiving scholarships courtesy of the NCC education endowment. Unfortunately, the school could not continue to operate in that manner, subsidizing student tuitions, and St. Rose of Lima Catholic School closed in 2007.

Still, New Community was very much in the business of education. With the burgeoning enrollment of students at our Workforce Development Center, and our day care and pre-school educational programs. I have been a student all my life; I received a PhD in Sociology from Fordham University in 1988. To embrace knowledge as life-altering and powerful is to never stop thirsting for it, because it reveals and delivers us unto ourselves. The power of education is as transformative as it is spiritual.

MONSIGNOR WILLIAM J. LINDER

CHAPTER 24

The Future of NCC

Trust in the Lord and do good that you may dwell in the land and live secure - Psalm 37:3

One of my earliest memories of my nephew Richard Rohrman is of an enterprising kid with a newspaper route. I remember driving down to my sister's house in Pennsylvania during a snow storm and the intensity of the storm making it nearly impossible for Rich to ride his bike to deliver the papers. I was impressed by his concern that his customers receive their newspapers. I told him I would drive him. At 12 years old, Rich's sense of responsibility to his customers was to be commended.

That kid with a newspaper route rose to the rank of executive director of New Community, taking over the reins of the corporation on April 1, 2013. I have the utmost confidence that Rich's ideas will best serve New Community as it moves into the future. Rich started here in 1981, in our maintenance division and helped me to implement a much needed work and purchase order system. It ensured that the right departments were being charged properly for supplies, equipment and services against the corporation. Rich involved himself from the ground up. Since then, he's held various positions within and outside of the company. His certification in property management and real estate development has been beneficial to us.

Newark has been my life ever since I first stepped foot in the city in 1963. Obviously, back then, I didn't know that something like New Community would ever exist. I did know that things could and should be better for the people who lived here in Newark. That was always first and foremost in my mind when New Community began to take shape. However, the time had come for me to step down from the day-to-day operations of the corporation. After all, I am not the young radical I used to be.

We're also in the process of restructuring our board of directors after the resignation of Art Wilson, who was chairman for 38 years. In the interim, I will assume the role as chairman until we find a suitable replacement. There's still too much work to be done for me to sit idle. Besides, it's not doing me any good and despite my physical limitations, I'll never stop doing what I do – loving all God's people. There is nothing more important in life than being loved. I am a vessel of God's love. You are who you are no matter what that is –the good, the bad and the ugly. All that we do at New Community is motivated by love.

Rich will pick up where I am leaving off and move New Community in not a new direction, but a better direction. We have a lot of equity in our real estate plus a chance to have some properties refinanced. Rich has been very aggressive in making this happen. Our real estate portfolio is aging but we mustn't lose sight, although a number of them are senior citizen residences, as we move into the future.

Therefore, we have to be smart in seeking ways to renovate them in a cost-efficient manner. Rich researched an energy-efficient initiative through PSE&G that allowed NCC to access an investment grade energy audit, at no cost. The audit alone would have cost us $30,000. With that energy audit, PSE&G worked out a program for New Community that upgraded the lighting, boilers and windows at our older properties, which in the long-run saves us money.

I truly believe we all come to this earth to do good things. Unfortunately, some lose their way and require the goodness of others to intercede and elevate humanity. New Community has been doing just this for close to fifty years. I am reminded of Ramon Rivera, who I met many years ago when he was the captain of the Newark chapter of the Young Lords, which could be described as the Latin version of the Black Panthers. Presumed to be a militant figure by the status quo, Rivera was a bonafide leader. He would often stop by St. Rose of Lima, where we engaged in informal chats. He just wanted to sit and talk about the state of affairs in Newark, but what he was really doing was formulating his vision and plans to develop a powerful institution. As the founder of La Casa de Don Pedro, a Newark-based community development corporation that serves the Latino community, Rivera elevated humanity in his leadership efforts to uplift his people.

Every day that I step across the threshold of New Community's headquarters, I am reminded of the task at hand: human development. New Community has never been just about bricks and mortar; human development has always been our greatest asset and strength.

Father Beatus Kitururu, a native of Kenya, who formerly taught psychology in our LPN program, explains the social fundamental of human development in his book: *The Spirituality of Hospitality: African and New Testament Perspectives.* "In its Latin root, *hospitalis* means, 'of the guest.' The guest is told to be 'free and relax.' Hospitality and bestowing freedom are inseparable. Respect, for instance, shows itself in greeting others. To pass another human being without a greeting is considered bad manners." Yet, we do this every day. Ignore one another.

Indeed, New Community has long been in the hospitality industry. The people we service are our guests. That can be said of the "Better Life" project that we've embarked on. It is near and dear to my heart, because it focuses on the most vulnerable guests- the mentally ill, some of whom are Vietnam veterans. It will consist of 24 units of housing, 20 of them being designated as permanent supportive housing units for the chronically homeless. The remaining four units will be used as temporary shelter. New Community is in partnership on this project with University Behavioral Healthcare, now part of Rutgers University. There will be very intensive services focused on the homeless who come through the emergency room on a regular basis. Often times they're in the emergency room for up to 18 hours where they are fed and then they're released, which is not doing anyone any good. So we're going to house them permanently and provide them with mental health, substance abuse and physical wellness services as needed. We're in the final phase of financing, so it looks as though we'll be able to start construction on the Better Life facility soon.

However, these days I only put in a few hours at the office. Although, being involved in the resurrection of St. Joseph Plaza was a joyful experience for me. Thanks to the creative wizardry of Jean Suggs, who helped with the design of the newly renovated space, along with the assistance of NCC Director of Environmental Services, Wayne Gravesande, the ecclesiastical structure is still beautiful, even more so now.

There are a number of areas in the corporation that can be embellished to strengthen the foundation of New Community to better serve the community in the future. For starters, the New Community Federal Credit Union, which operates now as a small town bank, is a place where members can access car, personal and mortgage loans. It has great potential, because it is a member of the Federal Home Loan Bank and it has the designation as a Community Development Financial Institution (CDFI). This puts it in another category that allows us to provide business loans, SBA loans, as well as tap into the Federal Home Loan Bank for low cost loans ourselves to use for redevelopment projects. Our credit union could be financing other entities for their projects, making it a go-to financial institution for real estate developers. We need to pull back on the retail operation that it has been and move in the direction of a larger operation, which would have a tremendous impact on the community and play a big part in economic development. This is one area that is already a work in progress.

We are also looking ahead to a program started for foreclosure projects. We'd like to partner with Victoria Foundation to analyze the condition of a few blocks in Newark and to fact- find who owns the properties and the condition of each and every house in the designated area. The point is to generate a plan that would revitalize the neighborhood. That's really how NCC got started after the '67 Summer Disorders. We focused on an area in the Central Ward and gave painstaking thought and analysis to the area that resulted in the development of a new community, a neighborhood that people could be proud of.

I have full confidence in Rich's ability to lead the company, after all he's been around me long enough to know he won't get very far accepting "no" from someone who can't give him a "yes." The blueprint for real estate development is already established. As long as we focus on the human development aspect, New Community will continue on the path that it has forged over the years – providing hope to the hopeless.

CHAPTER 25

A Network of Love

Iron is sharpened by iron; one person sharpens another
– Proverbs 27:17

The walls of the two conference rooms at New Community headquarters are filled with recognitions I have received over the years, far too many for me to name. Some of these awards are works of art, which makes for an interesting collection. Woven in between them are a number of photos taken of me with some powerful and famous people. One such photo is with Jane Fonda. That's a special one, because she's a person who uses her fame to bring awareness to causes. I was invited to do a series of workshops at the Carter Institute in Atlanta, Georgia, an organization that she and her then-husband Ted Turner supported. Jane was so impressed with my work that, along with a group of community organizers, she came to tour New Community, learn about community development and to personally thank me for the work I was doing. I'm humbled by every acknowledgment that has ever come my way. But above all else I see them as reflections of love.

Clearly, the beauty in being of service to others is the love that comes back to you. The installations of the four iconic steel sculptures by noted Netherland artist, Frederic Franck, were a beautiful gift of love to New Community. They symbolize a change in the environment, one in harmony with God and nature. In a 1995 interview in the *New York Times,* Franck referred to Newark as a "desolate" and "mauled city." A "Phoenix Rising" was an inspiring piece that Franck dedicated to me because of the change in the environment that had taken place in the Central Ward. A bird rising in flight stands out in a magnificent way at St. Joseph Plaza. Franck presented it to me himself. The beauty seen in the sculpted flower that adorns the front of New Community Harmony House, with its red-and-gold stained glass center, resurrects for those families who are transitioning from a homeless situation to one that is self-sufficient, that they are worthy. The other sculptures include, "Earth Mother" and "Child Out of Africa," that was on display in front of what was then Babyland III-day care center on South Orange Avenue. And "Seven Generations," represented a tenet of the Iroquois nation – you're responsible for what you inherit and what you pass on for seven generations. Its home is in between an elementary school and one of our senior citizen residences. The art is a reminder to find beauty in all things.

My lifelong journey of learning and understanding the colorful mosaic of cultures has enriched my world and led me to the discovery of how I could best serve God's kingdom by being a source of hope for all His people. My accomplishments in community and economic development have helped countless numbers of people. But more importantly, I've spread the word regarding community development through the many lectures I've given all around the world. I've also spread the methodology of community development by teaching as an adjunct professor at Rutgers and Columbia universities. The blueprint is there for transforming blighted urban communities into prospering environments. However, it does take a village to get it done. Everyone must participate

God's amazing grace continues to fuel my compassion and love for people. If we could only imagine a world where every sector of society came together to help out where help was needed, and not just during a crisis, that would lead to sustainable love. God-centered. Such a hope is the foundation of NCC. New Community grew as a corporation out of necessity, not for self-aggrandizement. We're here to be of service to others. Love brought everyone to the table in the beginning, even though some may not have seen it that way. That's the one thing that we all have in common we crave love. And if my priest's collar helped our effort, then I chose the right profession. Although there have been countless times when Kathy Spivey, my chief of staff, has had to remind me to wear my "dress blacks," otherwise known as my priest uniform, because I am a casual kind of guy. In many settings my priest collar seemed to make a difference while appealing to others to support NCC's efforts.

Sister Catherine Moran, a former NCC employee, used to say that I had a gift for bringing the right people together for a purpose. Again, I call it Divine intervention - God connecting me to a network of love. One such person would be Alfred A. Dellibovi, who made it possible for us to build many of our NCC homes, while he served as the deputy secretary of HUD from 1989-1992. That connection served NCC well, in addition to that of the Honorable Judge Jerome M. St. John, New Jersey Superior Court, who was NCC's number one volunteer. He provided us with countless hours of pro bono legal work and never expected any sort of compensation. It all comes down to this: How else do we experience ourselves as human if we do not extend compassion and love to our fellow man?

In the New Community pantheon of stories, Dr. Paul Kearney, who practiced pediatric medicine in the affluent area of Short Hills, was an important figure in our mission to help the most vulnerable of people, children. When a request went out for local volunteer pediatric doctors to provide services at the newly established Babyland daycare facility, Dr. Kearney was the only doctor to respond. He treated the babies at Babyland with the same compassion and care as the babies he served in the Short Hills area. After studying geriatrics, Dr. Kearney then became our medical director when the New Community Extended Care Facility opened. His devotion to our mission was a labor of compassionate love. NCC has been able to attract people such as Dr. Kearney in our mission to serve the poor and underserved of Newark.

Over the years, I've come to know quite a few people from every segment of the population. A great deal of what NCC has been able to do was predicated on the vision of others looking to make a difference in the city, from the philanthropic support of a couple, such as, Frank and Mimi Walsh, to corporations.

In 1978, Robert Beck, the CEO of Prudential, had the foresight to take the insurance giant beyond its traditional role of selling insurance. He steered the company, which has been steadfast in its financial support of NCC, in the direction of social change for Newark residents. NCC was actively engaged with the clientele of people that Prudential was looking to help. Our efforts to improve the quality of life for Newark residents fulfilled Prudential's mission to be of service to others. Donald Mann, then the senior vice-president of human resources for Prudential, chaired the advisory committee that helped to establish our Workforce Development Center.

Like Prudential, the Victoria Foundation is another entity that has been with us from the very beginning. In 1968, under the leadership of Percy Chubb II, the foundation's agenda included providing access to opportunities for residents in the Central Ward. It seemed that we were a perfect match for the foundation. Since then, NCC and the Victoria Foundation have maintained a meaningful relationship that has empowered people of Newark.

The NCC Workforce Development Center is the brain trust of the community, thanks to the help of the Victoria Foundation. It provided NCC with an $850,000 grant between 1992-1999 to help build the $4.5 million Workforce Development Center. To date, the center, has served close to 8,000 people. In 1998, under the umbrella of workforce and in an effort to create more jobs for those least likely to be hired – black and Latino men with a prison record – they were hired at NCC's Technology plant manufacturing components for nearly 1,000 homes and other new buildings.

Meanwhile, at the center, people can take preparatory classes for the GED exam in an atmosphere of continuing education. Students can choose from the Ford Automotive Training Center program, the New Community School of Practical Nursing - the first community-based Licensed Practical Nursing program in the nation - or the School of Culinary Arts, all accredited and leading to viable vocations. The increased value of the Victoria Foundation's love investment in the community is evident in the lives that are being changed every day for the better. The basis for economic development is investing in people.

A perfect example would be the 80 students who participated in the LPN capping and pinning graduation ceremony held at the New Community Neighborhood Center on Hayes Street, on July 17, 2013. The ceremony drew close to 400 people and included the proud parents and children of the graduates, along with other family members and friends. The graduating class represented the Americas, Africa and Haiti - all students of color-now prepared to escape the wrath of poverty.

I am grateful to the director of the nursing school, Ellen Boddie, for working tirelessly to get the program implemented and accredited. Since its inception in 2001, over 3,000 students have graduated from the 14-month intensive LPN program. Compared to other area LPN programs, some with tuitions as high as $30,000, NCC has managed to offer a first-rate program to our students for $13,000, with most of the tuition covered by the U. S. Department of Education/Pell Grant. This means our graduates, many of whom come from very low-income situations, are not hampered by the financial rut of student loans. Most of them will go on to obtain their Registered Nursing credentials that will buoy their success and self-sufficient status. Clearly, this is what economic development looks like.

The same can be said for the recent group of 25 job seekers who enrolled in our Ford Automotive Training Center program. Supported by a grant that NCC received from the Greater Newark Workforce Funders Collaborative for $100,000, many of these students were previously unemployed and undereducated. The yearlong program includes both classroom and hands-on instruction in a state-of-the-art technician center. Students also receive practical training by servicing NCC's fleet of vehicles, eliminating any need for us to outsource auto maintenance. Many of our students are placed in full-time positions at places such as Ford Motor Company Service Centers, Auto Land, Sansone Automall, Firestone Tire, Avis Car Rental, New Jersey Transit and Planet Honda. The total cost of the program is $7,500 again, totally covered by the U.S. Department of Education/Pell Grant with additional assistance from education benefits from the U.S. Department of Veterans Affairs.

Furthermore, our Culinary Arts Specialist program is a 30-week program that prepares students for entry-level positions in restaurants, hotels and other diverse establishments such as hospitals, nursing homes, cruise ships and colleges. A number of our graduates – Willie Robinson comes to mind – have gained employment at reputable establishments such as the posh "Winchester Garden" extended care facility in Maplewood. Others have been placed at fine dining establishments like The Grill at NJPAC, Maize Restaurant at the Robert Treat Hotel, Essex Fells Country Club, the Marriott Hotel at Newark Liberty Airport and the list goes on. Our interns gain practical work experience in food preparation working at the Culinary Café that is open to the public for lunch at NCC's Extended Care Facility. They then transfer that experience to commercial, institutional, cafeteria and fine dining environments after they graduate.

Through programs like these, New Community Corporation has improved the lives of thousands of inner-city residents while transforming much of the Central Ward into an attractive urban neighborhood. These programs are a major factor in maintaining the stability of the area. NCC will continue to empower low-income individuals to "determine their own destiny."

Over the years, I've had the opportunity to work with really dynamic people who have shared my same enthusiasm, concerns and interests for residents of the inner cities. High ranking officials from the state's community affairs agency have been good friends to NCC, starting with my dear friend Paul Ylvisaker, New Jersey's first Commissioner of Community Affairs, to former commissioners Jane Kenny (1999-2001) and Joseph V. Doria Jr. (2007-2009). NCC and other community development organizations have been assisted by public officials in improving the quality of life for people in New Jersey.

Commissioner Jane Kenny started the Urban Coordinating Council, bringing together officials from nearly all state agencies. The council was built on Kenny's conviction that urban problems are complex and necessarily cut across the jurisdiction of many agencies in government. Its activities focused on neighborhood-based strategies developed by community leaders. She was a real problem solver. And the same can be said for Doria, whose assistance with the demolition of Homes Court was invaluable.

Along the way I've also been inspired by others from around the country who have made great strides in their communities. People like Peter Garcia, the former president and CEO of Chicanos Por La Causa, Inc., based in Phoenix, Arizona. CPLC is among the leading producers of single-family and multi-family housing in the nation, and is a major force and advocate for Latinos. The more people we have lending their expertise to solving societal problems, particularly poverty, the better our chances of improving society.

The genesis of change can start with a housewife like Eleanor Josaitis, who along with Father William Cunningham, started FOCUS Hope in Detroit after that city experienced its own social upheaval back in the '60s. They developed a solid organization built around automotive and mechanical training programs that garnered the group a $100 million dollar grant. Garcia, Josaitis and Father Cunningham were change agents. We were a band of brothers and sisters. They gave me hope because they were out there doing great things to help the people in their respective communities, just as I was doing in Newark.

MONSIGNOR WILLIAM J. LINDER

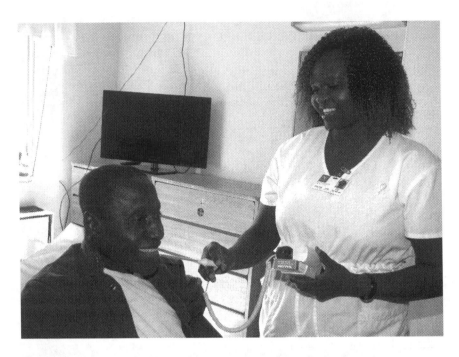

CHAPTER 26

Resurrecting *The* Church

You should love your neighbor as yourself - Mark 12:31

I believe the coronation of Pope Francis in 2013 represents a declarative change in the papacy. He is the first Jesuit to rise as Pope and from Latin America, another first. Unlike his predecessors, Pope Francis' main focus is missionary service when it comes to serving the poor and underserved. For far too long the church has operated from a canonical perspective governed by Canon laws, while the pastoral tradition has gotten lost. The more recent Code of Cannon Laws, according to Pope Paul II, was "in no way intended as a substitute for faith, grace, charisms, and especially charity in the life of the Church and of the faithful."

However, over the years the Catholic Church strayed away from this precept. Unlike years ago when you studied Canon law at the seminary, it has now become a degreed discipline. Many of the bishops of the church have their J.C.D. in Canon law. Basically, those who are ordained in the discipline are lawyers of the church and have little, if any, pastoral experience. That's been the recent culture of the church. However, Pope Francis' leadership is repositioning the church to match the architecture of the Vatican, and that is to open its arms to all people in a charitable way.

The thrust of my priesthood has centered on serving the needs of the people. The laws of the church were always secondary to charity. I recall being a young priest making rounds at the old Martland Hospital in Newark, where I would absolve, at their request, women who had opted for an abortion. The Roman Catholic Diocese of Newark wanted to know more details about the women. I told the diocese "That is none of your business." I was obligated by Canon law to tell the diocese how many absolutions I'd performed, but I saw no need for them to know anything else beyond that point. That's why my involvement with "Twenty Priests" was so controversial, because the archbishop at the time thought I was doing something improper and filed a case against me at the Vatican.

On the other hand, Pope Francis is leading differently, preferring that the church stay focused on the weak and the poor, healing and salvation. He is directing the church to get back to imitating Jesus as the pastor and spreading the gospel. When it comes to homosexuality, according to Pope Francis, the church shouldn't sit in judgment of that issue, although the emphasis on gay marriage is viewed by the church as weakening the institution of marriage. When it comes to the matter of abortion, Catholics believe that the unborn has life and are defenseless. Period. But what has weakened the church more than anything has been all the sexual abuse scandals. Not only did it expose the arrogance of those bishops and clergy who were implicated, but the church's cover-up by reassigning them to other parishes didn't help matters at all. Indeed, those who were guilty of the crimes should have been turned over and dealt with by civil law, and the church should have been aggressive in making sure others received clinical help.

It's going to take at least a century to change the canonical culture of the church, because it is so deeply ingrained. Pope Francis literally represents a cultural shift in the church, because the Vatican administers to the seminaries. That is where the change has to begin for the next generation of priests, who dare to answer the call to serve God and His people.

Jesus is the way. Perhaps one is inclined to follow the gospel of Jesus as a Baptist rather than a Catholic. Clearly, to believe in Jesus Christ and to have faith in Him as your savior is what matters. The idea of surrendering to Christ in faith has been put to the test time and again at New Community Corporation. A former employee, who happened to have been the CFO of NCC at the time, would be in a panic when we were going through difficult times financially, especially when it came to processing payroll. He once told my chief of staff, Kathy Spivey, that "if I were not a believer when I came to NCC, I've witnessed the impact of believing time and again." In the more than four decades that I have been at NCC, we have never missed a payroll, even in the most depressed times of the corporation. Kathy calls it "divine providence." In the midst of troubling times my faith in God has always remained strong. Unlike the typical office environment, the Monday morning water cooler chatter at NCC centers on Sunday's church service. It is during these times that we share scripture and engage in discussion. Kathy has often conferred with me about different passages in the bible as a way to better her understanding of the Lord's word.

The all-encompassing presence of the Lord is a way of life for me. And this has always worked in NCC's favor. When we were desperately seeking a communications director and editor for the Clarion newspaper published by NCC, within a week we received a resume from a highly qualified candidate who had been set adrift through attrition by the Star Ledger and was looking for employment. When you're assigned, as I have been, to do God's work, he'll make a way out of no way. But we must assign ourselves to be believers in God's Holy ordinance.

I believe this is the message that Pope Francis is delivering, while mandating that we must show compassion to the weak and the poor. In an article posted on CNN.com on October 4, 2013, Pope Francis criticized the idolatry of money with regard to corporate America's greed that has stripped the poor of their dignity. He said, "Where there is no work there is no dignity."

Dating back to Pope Leo XIII, who reigned as the oldest living Pope until his death in 1903 at the age of 93, he railed against a capitalistic society in which greed and wealth superseded the humanity of workers. He chastised the role of the state in "facilitating distributive justice," when it came to workers being paid wages that would sufficiently allow them to take care of their families. And this is still an issue today. New Jersey is one of the most expensive states to live in, yet Governor Chris Christie was against raising the minimum wage one dollar from $7.25 an hour to $8.25. It had to be put on the ballot in an election and it passed overwhelmingly. And the truth of the matter is that $8.25 is still not a decent living wage. Therefore, I wholeheartedly agree with Pope Francis' emphasis on making sure the poor are equally as favored as corporate America. He has already been referred to as the "most populist pope in our history."

With Pope Francis at the helm of the church, his leadership is steering the moral obligation of people in society back to believing in the teachings of Christ and to be our brother's keeper. Since the global phenomenon of the '80's, the prescript has been an individualist centered society. And clearly that's not been beneficial to all people. We see this in the staggering gap between the wealthy and the poor. Yet, I remain prayerful and hopeful that his papacy will resurrect what is human and decent in all of us and that is to "love your neighbor as yourself."

About the Author

William J. Linder retired from active ministry in the priesthood in Newark in 2012 after serving residents there for over fifty years. He holds a master's degree and PhD in sociology from Fordham University, and he is a renowned expert in the field of economic and community development. His mission is to help residents of inner cities improve the quality of their lives to reflect individual God-given dignity and personal achievement.

Printed in the United States
By Bookmasters